DECIDE FOR YOURSELF

A Theological Workbook

Gordon R. Lewis

INTERVARSITY PRESS
DOWNERS GROVE, ILLINOIS 60515

InterVarsity Press is the book-publishing division of InterVarsity Christian Fellowship, a student movement active on campus at hundreds of universities, colleges and schools of nursing. For information about local and regional activities, write Public Relations Dept., InterVarsity Christian Fellowship, 6400 Schroeder Rd., P.O. Box 7895, Madison, WI 53707-7895.

ISBN 0-87784-633-2

Library of Congress Catalog Card Number: 71-116046

Printed in the United States of America

38	37	36	35	34	33	32	31	30	29	28	27
13	12	11	10	09	08	07	06	05	04	03	

To my children . . .
Nancy, Cynthia and Scott
Stimulating fellow students
of the Scriptures

contents

After an adult Bible class a college graduate exclaimed, "I'm tired of being told what to believe!"

He spoke not only for himself, but also for me and many others. Though we respect theologians, we don't believe everything they say. On both sides of many questions there are equally dedicated experts. As thoughtful people, we must make up our own minds—and as Christians we must search the Scriptures to test the truth of what we hear.

Many Christians never leave the first principles of the gospel. Still spiritual infants, they must be bottle-fed the same formula. When confronted at the door by a representative of another sect, they are helpless to give a reason for the hope that is in them. On the basis of their faith they are speechless; yet on the reasons for their choice of a house or a car they can discourse at length. This sinful negligence by even one member of the church causes the whole body to suffer. Therefore, for the sake of our Lord and his Church, every Christian should develop his own convictions.

Jesus Christ calls his followers to a disciplined life—morally and intellectually. Lord of our minds as well as our hearts, he challenges us to grow, not in grace only, but also in knowledge.

This book is a response to the challenge to grow in knowledge. It is designed primarily for individuals who wish to investigate Christian doctrine on their own. It is a tool to be utilized—a guide for thinking through great Christian doctrines. Although the book is written for general readers —college students and adults—the material will also supplement reading assignments for theology courses.

I have adopted a standard procedure for research in each of the twenty-four studies. Each focuses on one basic theological problem and poses several possible answers. The reader is asked to determine which hypothesis consistently explains the greatest amount of biblical data with the fewest difficulties. On the basis of the evidence the reader formulates his own conclusion. And, finally, he considers the implications of his belief for daily living.

If you have reservations about considering the Bible as evidence or discovering knowledge about God, you may find the first three studies of special interest. They provide a logical starting point and show why the Bible is held to be the primary source and final standard of Christian thought.

Because of the extent of the biblical data it has been impossible to include all the references on a subject (except in Study 11). So the reader is free to consider any unlisted references that bear upon the questions considered. The listed references are selected because they are relevant to the issues and representative of other passages. Not all are equally obvious in their bearing upon the question asked. Some may even raise problems. Unless one is aware of such difficulties, and at least tries to resolve them, he has not adequately established *his beliefs.*

In deciding among controversial opinions, it is unwise to accept a position on the basis of one passage alone. The possibility of misinterpretation is too great. Such proof-texting has become notorious for serving unchristian causes. So, at the risk of appearing repetitious, I have listed several passages from different contexts to provide a more substantial basis for drawing your conclusion. The more of this evidence you can examine in context for yourself, the stronger should be the case for your conclusion.

Doing anything for oneself is sometimes hazardous and always demanding. For example, if a scientist is ever to see his experiment work out, he takes risks and disciplines himself. Our experience will be the same if we are ever to choose true and personally satisfying doctrinal commitments.

Here are a few hints before proceeding:

1. Use a large notebook with this study guide.

2. Answer each question by stating in your own words the precise point of each relevant passage.

3. Show how each belief you adopt derives from adequate Scripture. Don't be tempted to support a position with an out-of-context passage.

4. In formulating your final conclusion, review the background to the study and make a summation of all the Scripture you have investigated. Your statement should be the conclusion of this *study, not something from the past. Of course your conclusion may not be new, but it ought to be entirely yours.*

5. Once a belief is authenticated, trace its practical implications at length. The questions suggested in the section on "significance" are by no means exhaustive.

A word about the labels in the introduction to each study. Politically as well as theologically, party names may easily be misunderstood, for there are positions to the right and left in each classification. Names, while unavoidable, are not nearly so important as positions. Avoid merely verbal controversies. Rather than arguing against a stereotype of another's "Calvinism" or "Arminianism," "fundamentalism" or "neo-orthodoxy," drop the name calling and speak only of the carefully stated doctrines actually held.

If you want to be on the alert for my position, it is listed last in the background to each study. I confess that the discipline of formulating a basic problem precisely, stating alternative views on it succinctly, investigating the scriptural evidence minutely, expressing my own conclusions responsibly, and considering their significance for my life practically, has been most rewarding. I pray that it will be so for you.

Gordon R. Lewis
Professor of Systematic Theology and
Christian Philosophy
Conservative Baptist Theological Seminary

PART I

knowing God

1

Do all men know of God's creative power and righteous demands?

I. *Background*

Christianity is not a record of man's quest for God; it is the product of God's revelation of himself and his purposes to man. Since Christian convictions are founded on divine revelation, we must know to whom he reveals himself, what is taught, and how.

Has God manifested himself only to people who had contact with Israel, Christ, the Christian church and Scripture or has God made himself known equally to all men? Is God revealed only in great exceptional acts (miracles) or in the regular operations of nature as well? Is all knowledge of God conditioned on faith in Christ and new birth by the Holy Spirit, or may the unbeliever know something of God's power in creation and God's holy law in his heart?

These are momentous questions, the answers to which determine our view of the spiritual condition of outsiders to Christianity—whether they are the adherents of no religion at all or the sincere followers of other religions. Your answer to these questions determines how you view your relatives and neighbors who make no pretense of being Christian. Of course, on anything as sensitive as this, varied opinions have arisen.

A. According to some, nothing whatever may be known of God from nature. God is known only as his living Word, the eternal Christ meets an individual personally. To such divine-human encounters the Bible stands as a pointer or witness. Upon hearing that witness, men may come to know God personally. (Karl Barth) [1]

B. On the opposite extreme are those who hold that no special or direct acts of God are involved. All that may be known of God is obtainable indirectly through a study of man and nature. Every man has some knowledge of God, but the best theology is found in the highest achievements of human philosophy, science and psychology of religion. These correct the teachings of Scripture. (Liberals) [2]

C. Others maintain that all who will reason logically from their observations of nature must conclude that God exists. Apart from faith in Christ or any commitment to the Christian church, all may see that God is the uncaused cause of the world and its design. This knowledge creates a hunger for additional truth about God which is supplied by the authoritative teachings of the one true Church. (Thomists and others) [3]

D. Although God's existence and glory are plainly revealed to all men by the things that are made, some argue that men do not in fact see this because sin has blinded their minds to all spiritual truth. While there is a general revelation of God, there is no natural theology in the mind of the unsaved man. Only believers enlightened by the Holy Spirit can see God's glory in nature. (Reformed theologians)[4]

E. By the aid of a general illumination which enlightens every man who comes into the world, all men clearly see God's existence, power, and righteousness. In spite of their knowledge of God, however, none of them worship him as God. Instead, they worship and serve his creation. General revelation, like Moses' law, is holy, just and good, but because of the weakness of man's sinful nature, it results not in man's salvation, but his condemnation. And like the law it should then be a schoolmaster leading men to the saving grace of Christ. (Evangelicals)[5]

II. *Problem*
Which of the views on general revelation is most faithful to the biblical evidence? (To be answered in IV only after examining the evidence in III)

III. *Procedure*
In your own words state the teaching of relevant Scripture on the disputed issues.

A. Does God reveal himself at all in nature and man?

Ps. 19:1-6	*Rom. 1:19-20*	*Summarize.*
Acts 14:15-17	*Rom. 2:14-15*	

B. What may be known about God from the things he has made? What characteristics of God are revealed in nature?

Ps. 8	*Ps. 104:24*	*Rom. 1:32*
Ps. 19:1	*Ps. 148:13*	*Rom. 2:14-15*
Ps. 29:4	*Acts 17:24-29*	*Summarize.*
Ps. 93:1-4	*Rom. 1:20*	

C. Who perceives these characteristics of God in nature? All men? Or believers only?

Ps. 19:2-4	*Rom. 1:21*	*Rom. 1:32*
Rom. 1:18	*Rom. 1:25*	*Rom. 2:14-15*
Rom. 1:19	*Rom. 1:28*	*Summarize.*
Rom. 1:20		

D. What is the result of general revelation?

Rom. 1:18	*Rom. 3:10-11*	*Acts 17:27*
Rom. 1:20	*Rom. 3:19-20*	*Summarize.*
Rom. 2:11-12	*Rom. 3:23*	

E. Write out and memorize Rom. 1:20.

IV. *Your Conclusion*
State your doctrine of general revelation, incorporating and relating your answers to each question in III and clearly differentiating your view from others in I.

V. *Significance*
Think through the practical applicability of your study by answering the following questions.

A. Is any human being without some knowledge of God? Because of such knowledge is each man responsible? Are the references to Jews and Gentiles (Rom. 1:18—3:20) inclusive of the whole human race?

B. Does anyone always live up to the light he has?

C. Are all who have not heard the gospel lost? Are Jn. 3:18 and 36 a description of sinful man's continuing plight apart from Christ?

D. Are those who have not heard the gospel lost on the basis of not believing the gospel, or on the basis of rejecting light they do have (Rom. 2:12; Mt. 11:22)?

E. How can you make use of your conclusion on general revelation in witnessing to the unsaved? Consider Paul's approach (Acts 14:8-18; 17:16-34).

Notes

[1] Karl Barth, *Church Dogmatics,* II, 1 (Edinburgh: T. & T. Clark, 1957), pp. 63-254.

[2] Henry P. Van Dusen, *The Vindication of Liberal Theology* (New York: Charles Scribner's Sons, 1963), pp. 51-89; L. Harold DeWolf, *The Case for Theology in Liberal Perspective* (Philadelphia: The Westminster Press, 1959), pp. 19-41.

[3] Thomas Aquinas, *The Summa Theologica,* I, Q. 1, and 8-9; Fulton J. Sheen, *Philosophy of Religion* (New York: Appleton-Century-Crofts, 1948), pp. 123-176.

[4] G. C. Berkouwer, *General Revelation* (Grand Rapids: Wm. B. Eerdmans, 1955).

[5] Gordon R. Lewis, "Gospel on Campus: Based on an expository study of Acts 17," *HIS,* XXVII, Nos. 1-4 (October 1966-January 1967), No. 1, p. 14; No. 2, p. 24; No. 3, p. 11; No. 4, p. 34. Emil Brunner, *Revelation and Reason* (Philadelphia: The Westminster Press, 1946), pp. 49-80.

2

How may men know God's redemptive love and saving grace?

I. *Background*

Although general revelation makes available to all men a knowledge of God's power, righteousness, and providential rule, general revelation contains nothing of God's redemptive purposes through the incarnation of Jesus Christ. Apart from special revelation the wisest and most cultured of men have failed to discover gospel truth. But sinful men under condemnation need more than anything else to know of God's just and loving provision for their forgiveness.

God meets the sinner's need with "special" revelation. It is special in both content and outreach. Its content is not general truth about God but specifically God's gracious plan of redemption (including the centuries of Jewish history creating and preserving the Messiah's line). The outreach of special revelation, furthermore, is not universal but in fact limited to "many."

Among those theologians who hold that special revelation is necessary (Modernists did not), there are nevertheless serious differences. They do not agree on the way God makes known his reconciling love. Here are the leading positions:

A. God can be known as Savior through revealed *words*. The Bible is the written Word of God telling sinners about God and his grace. It is a love letter from heaven. (Some fundamentalists?)[1]

B. God can be known as Savior through miraculous *deeds*. God does not write a letter about his love for sinners, he demonstrates it! God's mighty acts more vividly reveal his purpose to save, than does any possible report of them. ("Biblical" theologians)[2]

C. God is known as Savior through personal *experience* of God himself. Far more significant than a love letter or a past demonstration of love, is the personal presence of the lover. God reveals his redemptive love by loving us. Sinners know God saves when they have a divine-human encounter. The Bible is human testimony to this person-to-person experience. (Neo-orthodox theologians)[3]

D. God cannot be known with face to face directness but is known as Savior only through the one true *church* established to interpret the Scriptures authoritatively. (Thomists and others)[4]

E. God is known as Savior, not through any one of the above emphases, but through a combination which includes: (1) revealed *words* interpreting miraculous *deeds* and asserting *truth* concerning the God who speaks and acts, (2) personal *experience* of God the Holy Spirit who "witnesses with our spirits," indwells, teaches, and leads every believer. Although the church is not a third form of revelation, it does enable a believer to check his understanding of God's redemption with other Spirit-illumined students of the Holy

Scriptures. (Evangelicals and fundamentalists)[5]

II. *Problem*
Which of the above views is most adequate? Why? (To be answered in IV only after examining the evidence in III)

III. *Procedure*
After a careful examination of relevant passages, answer questions arising out of the above views.

A. May men know God's redeeming love and power through miraculous *events* (mighty acts) in the context of Jewish history, the life of Christ, and the founding of the church?

Ex. 14:13, 31	*Dan. 6:26-27*	*Acts 14:3*
Deut. 7:18-19	*Lk. 1:49*	*Rom. 15:18-19*
Deut. 34:11-12	*Lk. 19:37*	*2 Cor. 12:12*
Josh. 24:17	*Jn. 5:36*	*Heb. 2:3-4*
Ps. 105	*Acts 2:19-21*	*Summarize.*

B. Is all divine revelation non-verbal, like a television program without the sound, or does God reveal himself redemptively through prophetic and apostolic *interpretations* of his mighty acts? Have we also *words* and *assertions* concerning the eternal God who acts?

1 Sam. 2:27	*Jn. 20:31*	*Jn. 14:6*
1 Sam. 3:21	*Rom. 16:25*	*Ex. 3:14*
Dan. 2:28	*1 Cor. 14:6*	*1 Pet. 1:16*
Is. 22:14	*Gal. 1:12*	*1 Jn. 1:5*
Mt. 11:25	*1 Tim. 3:15*	*1 Jn. 4:8*
Mt. 16:17	*Jn. 4:24*	*Summarize.*

C. Can one know God as Savior through Scripture apart from the enlightenment or "witness" of the *Holy Spirit*?

Rom. 8:9, 14-16	*2 Cor. 3*	*1 Jn. 3:24*
1 Cor. 2:10-16	*Gal. 4:6*	*1 Jn. 5:6-12*
1 Cor. 12:3	*1 Jn. 2:20-28*	*Summarize.*

D. Should a Christian ignore the Spirit-led interpretation

of other believers—particularly the central truths affirmed by the *church* through the centuries?

Acts 2:42, 44, 47	*1 Cor. 12:18-28*	*2 Tim. 2:2*
Acts 15:4-22, 25	*Eph. 3:17-19*	*2 Tim. 3:14*
1 Cor. 1:2	*Eph. 4:11-16*	*Summarize.*
1 Cor. 3:21—4:6	*2 Tim. 1:13-14*	

   E. Write out and memorize 2 Tim. 3:15.

IV. *Your Conclusion*
Summarize in your own words your view of special revelation showing how it agrees with and differs from other positions.

V. *Significance*
Consider the implications of your conclusion in terms of these questions:

   A. Should an institutional church claim special revelation from God for a tenet which contradicts the plain teaching of Scripture?

   B. Should a devout individual claim special revelation from God for a view which contradicts the plain teaching of Scripture?

   C. What attitudes and courses of action would you suggest for determining God's revealed will when conflict appears between what you understand to be the teaching of the Bible, the teaching of your church and the meaning of your experience of God?

Notes

[1] A view often attributed to fundamentalists by others, but not found in its scholarly works. However, the view may represent some unschooled opinions.

[2] G. Ernest Wright, *The God Who Acts* (London: SCM Press, 1952), pp. 1-132; G. Ernest Wright and Reginald Fuller, *The Book of the Acts of God* (Garden City, New York: Doubleday & Co., 1957).

[3] John Baillie, *The Idea of Revelation in Recent Thought* (New York: Columbia University Press, 1956).

[4] N. G. M. Van Doornik, S. Jelsma and A. Van de Lisdonk, *A Handbook of the Catholic Faith* (Garden City, New York: Doubleday & Co., 1956), pp. 137-152; J. Oliver Buswell, Jr., *A Christian View of Being and Knowing* (Grand Rapids: Zondervan, 1960), pp. 143-146.

[5] Bernard Ramm, *Special Revelation and the Word of God* (Grand Rapids: Wm. B. Eerdmans, 1961).

3

In what way is the Bible inspired and authoritative?

I. *Background*

Those who acknowledge special revelation hold that human language plays some part in it. Formerly prophets and apostles spoke for God. Today the Bible conveys his good news. The Bible is inspired—but in what way and with what results? How could finite, sinful men state in human language the undistorted truth of God?

In answering that question theologians differ widely on the meaning and significance of inspiration. Before examining the biblical data for yourself, consider some of the leading positions:

A. The Bible is inspired and authoritative because God dictated it audibly to human secretaries. Since finite and sinful men were passive and did not actively contribute to it, the

Bible is inerrant. (Some fundamentalists?)[1]

B. The Bible is inspired and authoritative because God prompted writers, who saw his mighty miracles and believed, to describe them for those who would not see and yet believe. Although not inerrant, these testimonies are authoritative like first-hand reports of an amazing victory in battle. ("Biblical" theologians)[2]

C. The Bible is inspired and authoritative because God prompted the authors who had experienced his presence to describe as best they could their encounter with the indescribable One. Although not inerrant, the Bible has the authority of one who knows by experience what he is talking about. It may evoke a similar experience in the reader. (Neoorthodox theologians)[3]

D. The Bible is inspired and authoritative because God providentially prepared the authors' personalities and writing styles, and supernaturally superintended the writing process so that their finite limitations and sinful biases did not corrupt any redemptive truth. Although there may be errors in matters not necessary for salvation, every statement comprising the primary redemptive plan is inerrant. (Some evangelicals)[4]

E. The Bible as originally given was inspired and authoritative because God providentially prepared the authors' personalities and writing styles, and supernaturally superintended the writing process so that their finite limitations and sinful biases did not corrupt anything God wanted written. Any scriptural statements, whether reports of events, encounters, or scholarly research, are as true as portions dictated by God. Whatever the Bible teaches on any subject is authoritative truth revealed by God. (Evangelicals and fundamentalists)[5]

II. *Problem*

Which view of the inspiration and authority of Scripture is

most adequate? Which do you hold? Why? (To be answered in IV only after examining the evidence in III)

III. *Procedure*

Study the Bible's view of itself, and answer the basic issues raised by the various views.

A. Do such passages as the following indicate divine dictation by an audible voice?

Ex. 4:12	*Num. 12:8*	*Isa. 6:8-9*
Ex. 19:3-6	*1 Sam. 3:4-14,21*	*Rev. 14:13*
Lev. 1:1	*1 Sam. 9:15*	*Summarize.*
Num. 7:89		

B. Were Bible writers ever eyewitnesses of events described?

1 Jn. 1:1-3	*Lk. 1:2*	*Summarize.*
2 Pet. 1:16	*Acts 1:21-22*	

C. Did the authors of Scripture sometimes write about their experiences of communion with God?

Ex. 24:1-11	*Ps. 42:1-2*	*Gal. 1:16*
1 Kings 22:19	*Ps. 84:1-2*	*2 Cor. 12:1-4*
Job 42:5	*Isa. 6:1-5*	*Summarize.*

D. Did God providentially prepare the prophets and apostles for their work as spokesmen for him?

Jer. 1:5	*Ps. 139*
Gal. 1:15	*Summarize.*

E. Were finite human beings completely passive or active instruments of God's communication with men?

Mk. 12:36	*Acts 28:25*	*Summarize.*
Acts 1:16	*1 Cor. 14:37*	

F. Did any Scripture originate with human initiative alone?

2 Pet. 1:20-21	*2 Tim. 3:16*	*Summarize.*

G. How did the Holy Spirit work with the writers of Scripture?

2 Pet. 1:21	*Zech. 7:12*	*Summarize.*

H. Do the claims of the New Testament imply that only some of the Old Testament is true and authoritative, or that all that it teaches is true and authoritative? Which view of the Old Testament was held by Christ and the apostolic writers?

Mt. 5:17-18	*Jn. 10:35*	*2 Tim. 3:16*
Lk. 24:25	*Acts 10:43*	*Rom. 15:4*
Lk. 24:26-27	*Acts 3:21-24*	*1 Cor. 10:6,11*
Lk. 24:44	*Acts 28:23-25*	*Summarize.*

I. Do the allusions of the New Testament to events recorded in the Old Testament imply that some detailed facts in the Scriptures may be in error or that all its assertions of fact are true? Which was the view of Christ and the apostolic writers?

Mt. 12:39-41	*Jn. 3:14*	*1 Cor. 10:7-10*
Mt. 19:4	*Jn. 6:31-33,49*	*Heb. 11:1-40*
Mt. 24:37-39	*Acts 7:1-53*	*Summarize.*
Lk. 17:28-32		

J. Write out and memorize 2 Pet. 1:20-21.

IV. *Your Conclusion*
Sum up in your own words the important elements of your view of biblical inspiration and authority, showing how it differs from other positions and why.

V. *Significance*
A. Those who defend inspiration may be charged with worshipping, not the living God, but a lifeless idol of paper and print. What would you say to that?

B. Discuss the popular statement that "our attitude toward God is shown in our attitude toward the Bible."

C. Should one who believes in the verbal inspiration of the whole Bible be any less diligent than others in maintaining personal fellowship with God?

Notes

[1] A view often attributed to fundamentalists by others, but not found in its scholarly works. However, the view may represent some unschooled opinions.

[2] C. H. Dodd, *The Authority of the Bible* (New York: Harper and Brothers, 1929).

[3] Emil Brunner, *Truth as Encounter* (Philadelphia: The Westminster Press, 1964).

[4] Daniel P. Fuller, "Benjamin B. Warfield's View of Faith and History," *Bulletin of the Evangelical Theological Society,* XI (Spring 1968), 75-83: Dewey M. Beegle, *The Inspiration of Scripture* (Philadelphia: The Westminster Press, 1963).

[5] Gordon R. Lewis, "What Does Infallibility Mean?" *Bulletin of the Evangelical Theological Society,* VI (Winter 1963), 18-27; B. B. Warfield, *The Inspiration and Authority of the Bible* (Philadelphia: Presbyterian and Reformed Pub. Co., 1948).

PART II

the living God

4

What is God like?

I. *Background*

According to religious polls nearly everyone believes in an ultimate power or fundamental reality on which everything else depends. Something, they think, is basic. But what? What are their Gods like?

For one retired high school French teacher, God is nothing other than "Mother Nature." Many think of God as an austere policeman driving right behind them to detect every fault. A former heavy-weight boxing champ thanks "the fellow upstairs," and a movie actress adores a "livin' Doll!" Steve McQueen, a Hollywood star, says "God is my kids, my old lady, green grass, trees, machines and animals."

Other views, possibly less sensational, represent various schools of thought:

A. God is a perfect, exalted man with a literal flesh-and-bones body. (Church of Jesus Christ of Latter-day Saints)[1]

B. God is eternal, impersonal Principle, Law, Truth, Spirit, and Idea. All that really is, is divine. God is spirit; there is no matter. God is good; there is no evil, sin, sickness or death. (Christian Scientists)[2]

C. God is totally unlike man, nature, or abstract principles. God is not like anything we know. We can only say, "God is not this," and "God is not that." We cannot say what God is. (Mystics)[3]

D. God is not physical, but spiritual; not dead, but living; not passive, but active; not impersonal, but personal. As a personal Spirit, God has intellect, emotions, and will. By virtue of these powers he can enjoy fellowship with persons created in his likeness. The living God acts in accord with his essential characteristics or attributes. (Orthodox Christians)[4]

II. *Problem*
How do you think of God? What view should you hold? Why? (To be answered in IV only after examining the evidence in III)

III. *Procedure*
From your own study of God's self-revelation, answer questions arising out of these differing concepts of God.

A. Is God "Mother Nature"? Any part or law of nature?

Gen. 1:1	*Heb. 1:10-12*	*Acts 17:24*
1 Kings 8:27	*Prov. 3:19*	*Summarize.*
Ps. 102:26-27		

B. Is God static and passive, or living and active?

Josh. 3:10	*Ps. 42:1-2*	*Jn. 6:57*
2 Sam. 22:47	*Ps. 84:1-2*	*2 Cor. 6:16*
Job 19:25	*Mt. 16:16*	*Summarize.*

C. Is God a perfected man with a flesh-and-bones body or an invisible Spirit?

Jn. 4:24	*Jn. 5:37*	*Col. 1:15*
Lk. 24:39	*1 Tim. 1:17*	*Heb. 11:27*
Jn. 1:18	*1 Tim. 6:16*	*Summarize.*

D. Does God possess the characteristics of impersonal principle or personal existence?

1. Intelligence; self-awareness; knowledge, wisdom, truth?

Ps. 117:2	*Acts 15:18*	*Heb. 4:13*
Jn. 21:17	*Rom. 11:33*	*1 Jn. 3:20*

2. Emotions?

Num. 11:1	*Ps. 7:11*	*Ps. 147:11*
2 Sam. 11:27	*Ps. 104:31*	*Lk. 15:7,10,22-24,32*

3. Will, self-determination, purpose?

Unconditional purpose with pleasure, never broken (Decretive will)

Isa. 14:24,27	*Dan. 4:35*	*Lk. 1:37*

Conditional purpose with pleasure, sometimes broken (Preceptive will)

Lk. 7:30	*Ex. 20:1-17*

Conditional purpose with displeasure, allowing evil, sin (Permissive will)

Ps. 81:12	*Rom. 1:24*
Acts 14:16	*Summarize this section.*

E. List additional characteristics of God taught in the following passages:

Ps. 90:2	*Ps. 92:15*	*1 Jn. 4:8,16*
Ps. 139:7-10	*1 Jn. 1:9*	*Ps. 116:5*
Ps. 99:3,5,9	*Ps. 86:5*	*Ex. 34:6*
1 Pet. 1:15-16		

Note that these qualities of God are not above God, in God, outside God, beneath God, or in any way apart from God. They belong to God and make him what he is. He does not act contrary to them. "He cannot deny himself" (2 Tim. 2:13). God is no arbitrary tyrant; God is holy, God is loving, God is gracious in all he does.

F. God's most perfect revelation of himself to the world

occurred in the life and ministry of Jesus Christ (Heb. 1:1; Jn. 1:14,18; 14:9). Think of instances in which Christ displayed the moral qualities of the Godhead to the world. Include a reference to as many as possible after each moral characteristic in E.

    G. Write out and memorize Ps. 84:2.

IV. *Your Conclusion*

In one paragraph, sum up all your findings about the nature of God, comparing and contrasting your view with others.

V. *Significance*

    A. What difference does it make how people think about God?

    B. What bearing does your concept of God have upon your desire for a devotional time each day?

    C. How does your way of thinking about God affect your reaction to reverses in life?

Notes

[1] Joseph Smith, trans., *The Book of Mormon,* Ether 3:6-16; James E. Talmage, *Articles of Faith* (Salt Lake City, Utah: The Church of Jesus Christ of Latter-Day Saints, 1952), pp. 36-48.

[2] Mary Baker Eddy, *Science and Health With Key to the Scriptures* (Boston: First Church of Christ, Scientist, 1932, Students' Edition), Chapter X, pp. 277-279; Chapter XIV, pp. 465-466.

[3] Walter T. Stace, *Mysticism and Philosophy* (Philadelphia & New York: J. B. Lippincott, 1960), pp. 277-306; William Braden, *The Private Sea: LSD and the Search for God* (Chicago: Quadrangle Books, 1967), pp. 15-45.

[4] Louis Berkhof, *Systematic Theology* (Grand Rapids: Wm. B. Eerdmans, 1946), pp. 1-81; A. W. Tozer, *The Knowledge of the Holy* (New York: Harper and Brothers, 1961).

5

Is God one? many? or triune?

I. *Background*

As people think about the unity or plurality of the fundamental reality on which all else depends, they arrive at divergent conclusions. The differences persist whether the source
of everything is viewed as personal or impersonal.

A. Impersonal views

1. Some judge that the great diversity of things in the
world requires *many* ultimate elements to explain it. But
their doctrine finds difficulty explaining the world's evident
unity. (Pluralists)[1]

2. Others argue that since the many types of things in the
world make up a *universe*, the ultimate source of everything
must be *one*. But difficulties arise when they try to explain
how from one and the same thing come so many different

things. (Plotinus and other monists)[2]

3. A third group seeks to avoid the problems of the first two by proposing a fundamental reality which is both *one* and *many*, a diversity in unity. Finding no better name, they call it the Absolute. But the Absolute is not a personal being. (Absolute idealists)[3]

B. Personal views (Theistic—from the Greek *Theos*—God)

1. Some hold there are *many* personal deities. They are called polytheists. They attempt to account for unity by regarding one God supreme over all the others, or by saying all are one in mind and purpose. (Animists, non-philosophical Hindus, Shintoists, Latter-day Saints)[4]

2. Others believe in but *one* personal Deity. They are called monotheists. They seek to explain multiplicity by the inexhaustible wisdom in the mind of God. (Jews, Muslims, Unitarians, Jehovah's Witnesses)[5]

3. A third group is trinitarian. There are not many gods; the Lord our God is one Lord. But within the one divine being exist three distinguishable Persons: Father, Son, and Holy Spirit. They share equally every divine characteristic and an eternally unbroken fellowship. Without in any way altering their oneness of essence and purpose, the three Persons fulfill distinct functions in the great work of redemption. The doctrine of the Trinity provides an ultimate explanation of multiplicity in unity which does not destroy personal existence. (Roman Catholics, Seventh-day Adventists, orthodox protestants)[6]

II. *Problem*
Which view of God best accords with all the evidence of divine self-revelation? Can you defend your conclusion? (To be answered in IV only after examining the evidence in III)

III. *Procedure*
Answer the questions arising from these divergent views on

the basis of a personal study of relevant Scripture.

A. Is polytheism scriptural? Are there many Gods or one?

Deut. 6:4-5	*Is. 45:18*	*1 Cor. 8:4*
Deut. 32:36-39	*Mt. 19:17*	*Jas. 2:19*
1 Sam. 7:22	*Mk. 12:32*	*Summarize.*
1 Chron. 17:20		

B. When the Bible asserts that God is "one" does it exclude the possibility of diversity in unity (of the Trinity) as monotheists insist? What kind of oneness is seen in the following passages—a single undiversified sameness or a plurality in unity?

Ex. 24:3	*Ezek. 37:19*	*Phil. 2:2*
Ex. 26:11	*Gen. 2:24*	*Acts 4:32*
Judg. 6:16	*Rom. 12:5*	*Summarize.*
Judg. 20:1,8,11	*Phil. 1:27*	

C. Is the Father God?

Mt. 11:25	*1 Cor. 8:6*
Rom. 15:6	*Eph. 4:6*

D. Is the Father a person with intelligence and will?

Mt. 6:8,32	*Mt. 6:10*	*Mt. 18:14*
1 Pet. 1:2	*Mt. 12:50*	*Summarize C and D on the Father.*

E. Is Jesus Christ a person united in thought and purpose with the Father?

Jn. 17:5,21-22,24

1. Intelligence

Jn. 2:24	*Jn. 16:30*	*Jn. 18:37*

2. Will

Lk. 22:42	*Jn. 6:38*
Jn. 5:30	*Jn. 17:24*

F. Is Jesus Christ merely a person in fellowship with God, or in addition to that, is Jesus essentially God, sharing the divine characteristics?

Mt. 1:23	*Jn. 20:28*	*Heb. 1:6,8*
Jn. 1:1	*Rom. 9:5*	*1 Jn. 5:20*

List divine attributes shared by Christ:

Heb. 1:11-12	*Jn. 21:17*	*Jn. 8:46*
Mt. 18:20	*Heb. 1:3*	*1 Pet. 1:19*
Mt. 28:20	*Heb. 13:8*	*Summarize E and F*
Jn. 16:30		*on the Son.*

G. Is the Holy Spirit a person with intelligence and will in communion (interceding) with the Father?

1. Intelligence

1 Cor. 2:10	*Jn. 14:26*	*Jn. 15:26*

2. Will

1 Cor. 12:11

3. Intercession

Rom. 8:26-27

4. Personal pronouns (though the word "spirit" in Greek is neuter)

Jn. 15:26	*Jn. 16:13-14*

H. Is the Holy Spirit merely a personal being in fellowship with God, or in addition to that is the Spirit essentially God, sharing the divine attributes? In the following passages is his name interchangeable with that of God?

Ex. 17:2-7 and Heb. 3:7-9	*Jn. 3:6 and 1 Jn. 5:4*
Isa. 6:8-10 and Acts 28:25-27	*Acts 5:3 and Acts 5:4*
1 Cor. 3:16 and 2 Cor. 6:19	

List divine attributes shared by the Spirit:

Ps. 139:7-10	*Jn. 16:13*	*Rom. 8:2*
Lk. 1:35,37	*Heb. 9:14*	*Summarize G and H*
Jn. 14:26	*Rom. 15:30*	*on the Spirit.*

I. Are there passages which associate Father, Son, and Holy Spirit in a way best explained by the doctrine of the Trinity?

Isa. 48:16-17	*2 Cor. 13:14*	*1 Pet. 1:2*
Isa. 61:1	*1 Cor. 12:5-7*	*Jude 20-21*
Mt. 28:19		

J. Write out and memorize Mt. 28:19 (note "name" is singular).

IV. *Your Conclusion*
How do you harmonize the Bible's teaching on the oneness of God and on the distinctness of the Father, Son, and Holy Spirit?

V. *Significance*
A. If Christ were not truly divine, of what would those who trust in him be guilty (Rom. 1:25)?

B. If the Son and Spirit are persons, is it possible to address prayer to them? Indicate ways to vary references to God in your prayers.

C. If you should not find adequate evidence to assert that God exists in three persons, could you with integrity sign a church's trinitarian confession simply for its emotive values?

Notes

[1] Frederick Copleston, *A History of Philosophy*, I, *Greece and Rome* (Westminster, Maryland: The Newman Press, 1953), pp. 47-53 and 463-75.

[2] *Ibid.*, pp. 61-80.

[3] *Ibid.*, pp. 463-475; G. Watts Cunningham, "English and American Absolute Idealism," *A History of Philosophical Systems*, ed. by Vergilius Ferm (New York: The Philosophical Library, 1950), pp. 315-327.

[4] Robert Brow, *Religion: Origins and Ideas* (Chicago: Inter-Varsity Press, 1966), pp. 1-54.

[5] *Ibid.*, pp. 55-88.

[6] *Ibid.*, pp. 89-123; Edward Henry Bickersteth, *The Trinity* (Grand Rapids: Kregel Publications, 1959).

6

Is life ultimately pointless or purposeful?

I. *Background*

In order to understand anything, said the Greek philosopher Aristotle (384-322 B.C.), we must know not only the material of which it is made, and the agent who made it, but also the purpose he had in making it, and the form he gave it in order to satisfy this purpose.

For centuries scholars sought to discern the purpose or sufficient reason of things. But modern science, so successful in discovering the materials from which things come, has failed to find reasons for their existence. On scientific methods they can describe what exists but not discover why it exists.

As a result, history seems to be "a tale told by an idiot full of sound and fury signifying nothing." The whole human race, like a cut flower, is destined to wither and die. Civilizations flourish and fade. Is there no purpose for all this shedding of blood, sweat and tears? We are told we should not ask *why*; that it is a question which cannot be answered. Unsatisfied to live in a pointless world, however, many seek to understand the purpose for which life exists on planet earth. What answers do they find?

A. Life is purposeful because all nature expresses an inherent principle of evolutionary progression both physically and culturally. Eventually the evolutionary process will bring utopia to earth, and we shall see the wisdom in it all. (Early twentieth century evolutionary optimists and Latter-day Saints or Mormons)[1]

B. Life is purposeful because all matter (and there is nothing but matter and its by-products) follows the inherent principle of dialectical progression. The conflict of opposites necessary to the dialectic will eventually produce an unending utopia on earth. Then the purpose behind history's painful struggles will be evident. (Karl Marx and communists holding to dialectical materialism)[2]

C. Life is, in fact, not fulfilling any ultimately meaningful ends or purposes. Evolutionary and dialectical guarantees of inevitable progress are pure fictions. Nature, now friendly to life on earth, will not always be so kind. Human history may end with the touch of a button unleashing nuclear power. In all this, no intelligent plan is discernible. But we ought not smother ourselves in self-pity; let us face up to reality as it is with "confident despair." (Bertrand Russell and many naturalists)[3]

D. No meanings can be found in time or eternity except those that human individuals themselves posit. The nonhuman is in itself simply meaningless. No God exists. What a man affirms must be invented each moment for human freedom has no basis or objective. A man keeps trying to move away from the absurdity of being-in-itself to the harmony of being-for-himself. But the attempt is futile. Man is a "useless passion." (Jean Paul Sartre and non-theistic existentialists)[4]

E. Nature and history have no objective purpose, but meaning is found in personal encounters. Life is purposeful in the presence of others when we do not withhold, but give of ourselves. The creative capacity of free persons is not absurd, but the gift of an absolute Thou. Life's supreme meaning comes in freely opening ourselves to God and others in inter-subjective experience. (Gabriel Marcel, theistic existentialists, neo-orthodox theologians)[5]

F. God's eternal purposes are disclosed, not only in personal encounters and mysterious deeds, but in verbal declarations of intent. According to the written Word, God's wise objectives encompass more than subjective encounters. Everything that exists in nature and that takes place in history fulfills some aspect of God's wise purposes envisioned in holy love. Temporary appearances notwithstanding, evil does not have the last word in the objective or the subjective world. All of life has meaning because all is ultimately related to divine justice and love. (Orthodox theologians)[6]

II. *Problem*
Which view of life's purpose is most biblical? Can you establish it with adequate evidence? (To be answered in IV only after examining the evidence in III)

III. *Procedure*
Since the living God reveals himself and his purposes through Scripture, the basic questions may be asked of the Bible's writers.

In the Bible, God's eternal purposes are designated by such terms as *decrees, counsel, establishment, ordination, favor, good pleasure.* An examination of these words in a complete concordance would be ideal.

Since earlier studies have indicated that God is not an

impersonal law of nature, the divine purposes cannot be identified with evolution or dialectic. What issues remain?

A. Is life on earth ultimately meaningless or in some way
related to the eternal purposes of God? Is there an over-
arching purpose behind nature?

Ps. 33:10-11	*Jer. 32:19*	*Eph. 1:11*
Isa. 14:26,27	*Dan. 4:35*	*Summarize.*

B. What has God revealed of his eternal plans and
purposes?

1. Why is there anything at all?

Ps. 104:24	*Prov. 3:19-20*	*Col. 1:16*
Ps. 135:6	*Prov. 16:4*	*Rev. 4:11*

2. Has God a plan in developments among the nations?

1 Chron. 17:9	*Isa. 14:24-27*
Ps. 76:10	*Rom. 13:1*

3. Does the divine plan permit evil?

Jer. 7:9,10	*Ps. 5:4*	*Jas. 1:13*
Ezek. 18:23,32	*Heb. 10:6,8,38*	*1 Jn. 2:16*
Ezek. 32:11		

4. Does God's purpose call for judgment of the wicked?

Jer. 49:20	*Zeph. 2:2*	*Heb. 9:27*
Jer. 50:45	*Heb. 1:12*	

5. Does God's purpose provide for man's redemption?

Acts 2:23	*Acts 4:27-28*	*Rev. 13:8*

6. Has God eternally purposed to save people through
faith in Christ?

Acts 13:48	*Eph. 1:3-12*
2 Tim. 1:9	*1 Cor. 2:7*

7. Can the redeemed share in achieving the divine objectives?

Jer. 1:5	*Ps. 73:24*	*Rom. 9:11*
Jn. 15:16	*Eph. 2:10*	

8. Has God planned the culmination of history?

Isa. 46:10	*Jer. 33:25-26*	*Heb. 6:17-19*
Isa. 55:10-11	*Acts 15:18*	*Summarize this section.*

C. While Christians agree that God purposes to save people (previous point 6), they differ significantly as to whether or not God chooses particular individuals and as to the basis of that choice.

Some who follow Jacobus Arminius (1560-1609) think that God did not choose individuals to be saved, but merely the class of all who would trust Christ. From eternity God foreknew those who would believe and called them his elect. (Methodists, many Pentecostalists, many Baptists)

According to others who follow John Calvin (1509-1564), God foreknew that no sinner would accept Christ. So God chose "many" to receive the gift of faith in order to secure his saving purposes. (Presbyterians, Reformed, many Baptists)

1. Did God, before the foundation of the world, choose to save certain individuals or the class of those who would believe on Christ?

Jn. 6:37-40,44,65   *Jn. 13:18*   *Jn. 17:2,6,9,11,12,24*
Jn. 10:26-29   *Jn. 15:16*   *Eph. 1:3-12*

2. Is the divine choice based on the foreseen faith of men (Arminianism) or on the purposed gift of faith by God (Calvinism)?

　　a. Passages utilized by Arminians in support of foreknowledge as the basis of election include:

Rom. 8:29   *1 Pet. 1:2*

　　b. Passages used by Calvinists to teach that divine foreknowledge includes pre-determination as well as pre-knowing include:

Rom. 11:2   *1 Pet. 1:20*   *Acts 2:23*

　　c. Passages indicating to Arminians that faith is possible for sinners include all the "whosoever wills" and all the commands to believe on Christ and accept him:

Jn. 3:16   *Acts 10:43*   *1 Jn. 3:23*
Jn. 6:47   *Acts 16:31*   *1 Jn. 5:1*
Acts 2:21   *Rom. 10:11-13*

d. Passages which make Calvinists think that faith is possible for sinners only by a special gift of God's grace include:

1 Cor. 12:3	*Phil. 1:29*	*Eph. 6:23*
Acts 13:48	*1 Cor. 12:9*	*2 Thess. 2:13*
Eph. 2:8	*Rom. 12:3*	

3. What is your judgment regarding God's eternal purpose to save people through Christ? Do you incline toward Arminianism or Calvinism? Show how you relate the teaching of Scripture in a. and b., c. and d.

D. Write out and memorize Jn. 6:37.

IV. *Your Conclusion*

In your own words answer the question: "Is life ultimately pointless or purposeful?" Indicate where you differ from other views on the subject.

V. *Significance*

A. Should the doctrine of divine decrees bring fear, resentment and lethargy, or confidence, blessing and consecrated service?

B. Can nuclear destruction wipe out the human race contrary to the purposes of God?

C. Should the differences between Calvinists and Arminians on election be made a test of Christian fellowship?

Notes

[1] Carl F. H. Henry, *Remaking the Modern Mind* (Grand Rapids: Wm. B. Eerdmans, 1946).

[2] Karl Marx and Frederick Engels, *Manifesto of the Communist Party* (Moscow: Foreign Languages Publishing House, 1955); Gustav A. Wetter, *Dialectical Materialism* (New York: Frederick A. Praeger, 1958), pp. 375-396.

[3] Bertrand Russell, "Hope," *Bertrand Russell's Dictionary of Mind, Matter and Morals,* ed. by Lester E. Denoun (New York: The Philosophical Library, 1952), p. 93.

[4] Jean Paul Sartre, *To Freedom Condemned: A Guide to His Philosophy* (New York: Philosophical Library, 1960).

[5] On Gabriel Marcel see David E. Roberts, *Existentialism and Religious Belief* (New York: Oxford University Press, 1957), pp. 275-332.

[6] Emilie Cailliet, *The Recovery of Purpose* (New York: Harper and Brothers, 1959); Louis Berkhof, *Systematic Theology* (Grand Rapids: Wm. B. Eerdmans, 1946), pp. 165-178.

Part III

God's world

7

Does everything come from God?

I. Background

By and large modern scientists will not ask, let alone answer, the question of ultimate origins. Evolution as popularly held always begins with something: a bit of protoplasm on the surface of a primeval pool, gases, a whirling mass of matter, or a few suns. Where these came from scientists have no way of knowing. They are to be commended for avoiding such speculation as that of the American philosopher Charles Sanders Pierce who supposed that

> In the beginning—infinitely remote—there was a chaos of unpersonalized feeling, which being without connection or regularity would properly be without existence. This feeling, sporting here and there in pure arbitrariness, would have started the germ of a generalizing

tendency. Its other sportings would be evanescent, but this would have a growing virtue. Thus the tendency to habit would be started; and from this with the other principles of evolution, all the regularities of the universe would be evolved.[1]

Contemporary theologians have been as reticent as scientists to speculate about origins, preferring to leave such matters of fact to the scientists, and to be silent where they are silent. Paul Tillich, for example, understands the Bible's references on creation to teach, not an ancient fact, but a present quality of our existence. "The doctrine of creation," Tillich explains, "does not describe an event. It points to the situation of creatureliness and to its correlate, the divine creativity."[2] Our very existence from day to day is utterly dependent upon God. That is the sole point of the Christian doctrine of creation, many contemporary theologians inform us.

Not everyone is so cautious in speaking about the source of the universe. What are some alternative views?

A. The universe had no beginning. It is essentially matter, and matter is eternal. (Dialectical materialists, communists)[3]

B. The universe had no beginning. It is essentially divine, necessarily and eternally emanating from God as light continuously flows out from the sun. (Pantheists, neo-platonists, absolute idealists)[4]

C. The universe had a beginning; its basic elements arose spontaneously out of nothing. (Popular atheistic evolutionists)[5]

D. The universe had a beginning, and "in the beginning was not chaos; in the beginning was God." (Erich Sauer) Creation was a part of God's grand design from all eternity. Until the first creative word was freely spoken, there was nothing but the triune God. Then a vast universe came to be according to the will of God. The Bible reveals that creative events took place, but it reveals little of the way in which

God brought them to pass. A distinction is made, however, between the initial act (immediate creation out of nothing), and subsequent creative acts employing materials of the first act (mediate creation). (Orthodox Christians)[6]

II. *Problem*
Which view of ultimate origins is most biblical? (To be answered in IV only after examining the evidence in III)

III. *Procedure*
Answer the questions arising out of these divergent positions on the basis of a Spirit-illumined study of relevant Scripture.

A. Did the universe, including matter, have a beginning?

Gen. 1:1	Jn. 1:1-3
Ps. 90:2	Summarize.

B. Did the stuff (raw material) of the universe arise spontaneously out of nothing, or did it come from God?

Gen. 1:1-2	Rom. 11:36	2 Cor. 5:18
Heb. 11:3	1 Cor. 11:12	Summarize.

C. Are all things "out of" God by a process of emanation or by a free act of God's will expressed in his Word?

Ps. 33:6,9	Jn. 1:1-3	Summarize.
Ps. 148:5	Heb. 11:3	

D. In addition to the initial creative act (Gen. 1:1-2, the immediate creation *ex nihilo*), what other creative acts are mentioned? List the things said to be created or made on each day (Gen. 1:3–2:3, mediate creation).

E. Did God employ any existing materials in creating the various things of Gen. 1:3–2:3? (See Gen. 2:7 and consider why the term "make" is employed synonymously with "create" in these passages.)

F. How many times does "after its (their) kind" occur in Gen. 1 and 2? How would you define "kind"? With which, if any, of the following scientific classifications would you identify the "kinds" of Genesis?

Kingdom	Order	Genus
Phylum	Family	Species
Class		

(If unfamiliar, these designations may be looked up in an encyclopedia under "classification.")

G. How much time elapsed between the mediate creative acts? How long were the "days"? 24 hours? A great age of undetermined length? Check a concordance on uses of "day" in the Old Testament, preferably a complete concordance. Those who argue for 24 hours say the word usually means that, and emphasize Ex. 20:11. Those who argue for a long period of time say the word also means more than 24 hours in many contexts: Gen. 2:4; Josh. 24:7; 2 Chron. 15:3 translated "season," Lev. 25:8 "space." See also 2 Pet. 3:8. "Evening" and "morning" are also used for longer periods of time: Jer. 6:4, see 1-6; Ezek. 7:7-10; Ps. 90:5-6. (See Scofield Bible notes on Gen. 1:5.) How long, in your opinion, were the "days" of the creation account before the fourth day and after the fourth day (Gen. 1:14-19)?

H. Write out and memorize Heb. 11:3.

IV. *Your Conclusion*

State in your own words your view of ultimate origins, clearly differentiating it from other views.

V. *Significance*

A. Can we believe that God is in complete control of the forces of our universe now, if he was not at its origin?

B. Is matter evil in itself? Is the physical body evil in itself (1 Tim. 4:4-5 and 1 Cor. 3:21-22)?

C. Should you regard any person, animal or thing as your highest object of concern? On the other hand, should you despise any person, animal or thing God created?

Notes

[1] Charles Sanders Pierce, "The Architecture of Theories," *The Monist,* I (January 1891), 161-176, reprinted in Max H. Fisch, *Classic American Philosophies* (New York: Appleton-Century-Crofts, 1951), p. 99.

[2] Paul Tillich, *Systematic Theology,* I (Chicago: The University of Chicago Press, 1951), pp. 252-253.

[3] Gustav A. Wetter, *Dialectical Materialism* (New York: Frederick A. Praeger, 1958), p. 292.

[4] Plotinus, *Enneads,* IV, 8; V, 1, 2, 3, 4, 9; Emile Bréhier, *The Philosophy of Plotinus* (Chicago: The University of Chicago Press, 1958), pp. 43-52.

[5] G. A. Kerkut, *Implications of Evolution* (New York: Pergamon Press, 1960), pp. 6-7 and 150-157.

[6] John Gill, *Body of Divinity* (Atlanta, Ga.: Turner Lassetter, 1957 reprint), pp. 256-262; Bernard Ramm, *The Christian View of Science and the Scripture* (Grand Rapids: Wm. B. Eerdmans, 1954), pp. 65-122.

8

Does everything take place according to the will of God?

I. *Background*

Apparently the founders of the state of Colorado believed that everything takes place according to God's will. The state motto affirms: *Nil sine Numine*, "Nothing without Providence." And the Colorado state seal pictures the all-seeing eye of God. Can we today believe that everything in our state, nation and world fits into the divine plan? Are God's eternal purposes actually being achieved on our perplexing globe? How could they be? Opinions vary.

    A. Some think God achieves his purposes indirectly through the general laws of nature established at creation. There are no exceptions. Since the beginning the First Cause has taken no direct action in nature or history. (Deists)[1]

    B. Everything takes place according to the "will" of God because everything is part of God. God is the unity of all that is real. Dynamic reality in its wholeness is divine. (Pantheists, some liberals)[2]

C. Now that the inevitability of evolutionary progress has been exploded by two world wars and atomic bombs, many contemporary theologians have conceded that nature and history seem purposeless and relegate the achievement of divine purposes to the hearts of believing men. God's Lordship is spiritual and subjective only. (Religious existentialists and neo-orthodox theologians)[3]

D. God's purposes in the world often include judgment as well as evident progress. Whether we can or cannot see them, the Creator's plans are being realized through general laws of nature, specific historical events, organisms and the inner will of human beings. In some areas God's will is accomplished decretively, in some preceptively, and in others permissively (See Study Guide 4). (Orthodox Christians)[4]

II. *Problem*
How should we think of God's relation to the world of nature and human history? Which view merits your assent? Why? (To be answered in IV after examining the evidence)

III. *Procedure*
Answer questions arising out of these differing viewpoints on the basis of your own investigations of relevant Scripture.

A. God, as already established (Study Guide 4), is distinct from nature and its laws. Does nature with its laws exist and function, then, apart from divine preservation and government? Or do the observable regularities of nature fulfill God's purposes?

Gen. 8:21-22	*Ps. 104:1-35*	*Col. 1:16-17*
Ps. 24:1	*Ps. 135:5-7*	*Heb. 1:3*
Ps. 95:4	*Neh. 9:6*	*Summarize.*
Ps. 103:19	*Acts 14:17*	

B. Does God also achieve his purposes in particular events and specific details of life?

1 Sam. 2:6-10	*Ps. 66:5-7,12*	*Lam. 2:17*
Ps. 22:28	*Ps. 75:6-7*	*Mt. 10:29-31*
Ps. 33:10-11	*Prov. 16:33*	*Summarize.*

C. Does God accomplish his purposes in the hearts of men—unbelievers as well as believers?

Ex. 12:36	*Prov. 21:1*	*Jer. 10:23*
1 Kings 12:12-24	*Prov. 16:9*	*Phil. 2:13*
Ps. 47:8	*Prov. 19:21*	*Summarize.*

D. How does God's providential agency relate to the good acts of men?

1 Cor. 4:7	*Eph. 2:10*	*Jas. 1:17*
2 Cor. 12:9-10	*Phil. 2:13*	*Summarize.*
Gal. 5:22-25	*Phil. 4:13*	

E. How does God's providential agency relate to the evil acts of men?

1. Does God prevent evil from occurring?

Gen. 20:6	*Ps. 19:13*
Gen. 31:24	*Hos. 2:6*

2. Does God will evil to occur? If so, in what sense?

2 Chron. 32:31	*Deut. 13:3*	*Rom. 1:24*
Deut. 8:2	*Acts 14:16*	*Rom. 1:28*

3. Does God limit and restrain evil that has been permitted?

Job 1:12	*Ps. 124:2*	*2 Thess. 2:7*
Job 2:6	*1 Cor. 10:13*	*Rev. 20:2-3*

4. Does God overrule evil to accomplish good?

Gen. 45:5	*Ps. 76:10*	*Acts 3:13-15*
Gen. 50:20	*Acts 4:27-28*	*Rom. 8:28*

5. What specific good was accomplished through evil or suffering in the following cases?

Hos. 4:1-3	*Jn. 11:6-15*	*Mt. 5:10-12*
Heb. 12:5-11	*Ps. 119:67,71*	*Summarize this section.*
Jn. 9:3	*Acts 4:1-4*	

F. Write out and memorize Eph. 1:11.

IV. *Your Conclusion*
As a result of your study answer in your own words this question: Does everything in the world take place according to the will of God?

V. *Significance*
A. Do you agree with John Calvin that the doctrine of divine providence produces: (a) praise in prosperity, (b) patience in adversity, and (c) peace for the future?
B. What effect of providential goodness should follow according to Rom. 2:4?
C. Why do you think this teaching so often seems offensive rather than comforting?

Notes

[1]Thomas Paine, *The Age of Reason* (New York: G. P. Putnam's Sons, 1896), pp. 21-23 and 83-84.

[2]Alasdair MacIntyre, "Pantheism," *The Encyclopedia of Philosophy* (New York: The Macmillan Co. and the Free Press, 1967), pp. 31-35; Harvey H. Potthoff, *God and the Celebration of Life* (Chicago: Rand McNally, 1969), pp. 184-196.

[3]Langdon B. Gilkey, "The Concept of Providence in Contemporary Theology," *The Journal of Religion,* XLIII (July 1963), 171-192.

[4]G. C. Berkouwer, *The Providence of God* (Grand Rapids: Wm. B. Eerdmans, 1952); William G. Pollard, *Chance and Providence* (New York: Charles Scribner's Sons, 1958).

9

How effective is prayer?

I. Background

Apparently, many think of prayer as a handy thing to have around in time of trouble. But confidence in the effectiveness even of "foxhole praying" may be waning. A popular newsmagazine reports, "Many people no longer pray to God to change events." One hears fewer and fewer "gimme, gimme" prayers.

People are learning, we are told, that prayer is far more than "a summary demand for divine action." And indeed it is. According to the Bible prayer may take the form of adoration, praise, communion, waiting upon God, hearing God speak, receiving divine guidance, fellowship with God, self-examination before God, confession, repentance, meditation and worship. Prayer, like love, is a "many-splendored thing."

But broad as our view of prayer may be, we cannot escape a recurring question. Does prayer really affect anything in the world of fact? If God's purposes are eternally unchanging, what good does it do to pray? Since the omnipotent God does as he pleases in the world, why pray? In view of providentially sustained regularities of nature, prayer seems pointless. Is it? Judgments differ.

A. Prayer can affect only the one who prays, some think, by a kind of auto-suggestion. Even in a closed system of natural causes prayer may be a psychological therapeutic releasing subjective tensions and inducing healthy attitudes toward life. (Some liberals)[1]

B. For a different reason others also hold that prayer (actual communion with God) affects only the one who prays. Such fellowship with the living God of heaven and earth cannot leave the devout unchanged. (Neo-orthodox theologians)[2]

C. Prayer, according to some, can change not only the one who prays, but also the spiritual world surrounding him. On this view prayer for changes in the weather are futile since weather conditions are based on certain atmospheric antecedents. However, since God can act in the mental and spiritual realms, we might reasonably pray for the psychosomatically ill. Intercessory prayer helps establish a community-in-love. (Personalists)[3]

D. And many believe prayer can affect not only the one who prays and the spiritual world, but also the physical world. Just as intelligence may direct the body, God may, in answer to prayer, direct any part of nature. God's eternal purpose was not to exclude human petition, but to grant certain things only in answer to prayer. His omniscience takes the faintest prayer into account. And providentially prayer has power over all that over which God himself has power. This view, like the previous ones, may be held in two very different ways:

1. As a form of *magic* prayer may be thought to compel God to do what we want. Invariable "success" alone could substantiate this view of prayer. (Characteristic among the immature and superstitious)

2. As a *request* to an all-wise God prayer may or may not be granted. God may say "Yes," "No," or "Not yet." Since God chooses to respect his children's requests, it is no more strange that my prayer should affect events than that my other actions should do so. (Orthodox Christians)[4]

II. *Problem*
Which view of the effectiveness of prayer should a Christian hold? Why? (To be answered in IV only after examining the evidence in III)

III. *Procedure*
Answer questions prompted by these different positions, after studying relevant Scripture.

A. In what ways can prayer affect the one who prays?

Ps. 118:5-6	*Dan. 9:20-27*	*Jn. 16:23-24*
Ps. 138:3	*Joel 2:32*	*Phil. 4:6-8*
Isa. 58:9-11	*Mt. 6:6*	*1 Pet. 5:7*
Lam. 3:57	*Lk. 11:13*	*Summarize.*

B. Can prayer be spiritually effective in relation to others? How?

2 Chron. 7:14	*Phil. 1:9-11*	*2 Thess. 2:16-17*
Job 33:26	*Col. 1:9-12*	*2 Thess. 3:5*
Mt. 6:10	*1 Tim. 2:1*	*Philem. 6*
Eph. 1:18-19	*1 Thess. 3:10-13*	*Heb. 13:20-21*
Eph. 3:16-21	*2 Thess. 1:11-12*	*Summarize.*

C. Can prayer also be effective in the physical world?

1 Chron. 4:10	*Jonah 2:7-10*	*1 Thess. 5:23*
Ps. 34:15-22	*Mt. 6:11*	*Jas. 5:13-18*
Ps. 65:2,5	*Acts 4:31*	*Summarize.*
Prov. 30:7-9	*Acts 16:25-26*	

D. For what reasons are requests sometimes refused?

Ps. 66:18	*Jer. 14:10-12*	*Heb. 11:6*
Prov. 28:9	*Mal. 1:7-9*	*Jas. 1:6-7*
Isa. 29:13	*Mt. 6:5-6*	*1 Pet. 3:7*
Isa. 59:2	*Lk. 18:11-14*	*Summarize.*

E. Since prayer is not effective by its own virtue, what conditions contribute to a favorable hearing of requests?

Isa. 58:6-9	*Lk. 18:1-8*	*1 Jn. 3:22*
Mk. 11:22-24	*Jn. 14:13-14*	*1 Jn. 5:14-15*
Mk. 11:25-26	*Jn. 15:7*	*Summarize.*
Lk. 11:5-10	*Eph. 6:18*	

F. Are the requests of the righteous which would apparently meet all the conditions of answered prayer necessarily granted?

Mt. 26:36-44   *2 Cor. 12:8-9*

G. Should we, even when convinced of our own integrity in meeting the conditions of answered prayer, insist on our own way?

Ps. 106:15   *Job 6:8-9*

H. Write out and memorize Jas. 5:16.

IV. *Your Conclusion*
In your own words answer the question, "How effective is prayer?"

V. *Significance*
A. To an omniscient God is there any such thing as an unanswered prayer?

B. What would happen if all requests were granted as asked?

C. Is there a difference between answering a request and a man, that is, between answering a particular petition and the dominant purpose of a man?

D. What pre-requisites does a wise father require of his sons before granting them their share of the inheritance?

Notes

[1] James A. Kirk, "Prayer and Personality," *Iliff Review*, XIX (Spring 1962), 23-27; Harvey H. Potthoff, *God and the Celebration of Life* (Chicago: Rand McNally, 1969), pp. 247-250.

[2] Emil Brunner, *The Christian Doctrine of the Church, Faith, and Consummation* (Philadelphia: The Westminster Press, 1960), pp. 324-335; Karl Barth, *Church Dogmatics* (Edinburgh: T. & T. Clark, 1956), I/2, pp. 697, 755; II/1, pp. 26, 512, 697; II/2, p. 194; IV/1, pp. 355, 576-577; IV/2, p. 643.

[3] Peter Anthony Bertocci, *Introduction to the Philosophy of Religion* (Englewood Cliffs, N. J.: Prentice-Hall, 1951), pp. 469-496.

[4] C. S. Lewis, "The Efficacy of Prayer," *HIS*, XIX (May 1959), 6-8; C. S. Lewis, *Letters to Malcolm: Chiefly on Prayer* (New York: Harcourt, Brace & World, 1964); Gordon R. Lewis, "Prayer," *Zondervan Pictorial Bible Encyclopedia* ed. by Merrill C. Tenney (Grand Rapids: Zondervan, forthcoming).

PART IV

man against God

10

What is man?

I. *Background*

"Man is what he eats!" So say materialists. But Jesus said, "Man shall not live by bread alone." Created by God to fellowship with him, man is more than an animal.

But the Bible does not minimize man's body. One topical index lists passages on the outward man under the following headings: the unity of the body, manly beauty, female beauty, diminutive stature, giants, dexterity, the five senses, the appetites, the countenance, the hair, the beard, the forehead, the eyes, the ears, the mouth, the teeth, winking, stooping, prostration, sighing, tears, saliva, excretions, necessity of food, varieties of food, cooking, feasting, gluttony, fasting, famine, drink, abstinence from wine, wine-drinking, drunkenness, sleep, body clothed, folly of anxiety about dress, directions to women, material of dress, color of material, portions of dress, seemliness of dress, ornaments of dress, garments perfumed, disguised by dress, grief exhibited by dress, removal of dress, afflictions of the body, sickness, weakness, restlessness, pain, consumption, fever, palsy, leprosy, cutaneous disorders, sores and boils, mutilation, wounds, lameness, sun-stroke, blindness, pestilence, physicians, prescriptions, apothecaries, sickness caused by sin, recovery is of God, old age promised, vigorous old age, feeble old age, duties of the aged, duties to the aged, instances of longevity, death the ordering of God, an appointed time to die, all must die, fraility of life, uncertainty of life, brevity of life, preparing for death, instances of death, burying the dead, grief for the dead, sympathy with the mourners, burials, the grave monuments, corruption, non-burials, bodies devoured, bodies burned.

There can be little question about the reality and importance of the outward man. Is man more than this? If so, what is the relationship of the "something more" to man's body? Views differ.

A. Some think man is nothing but a body. After death nothing personal of the man continues to exist. (Materialists)[1]

B. At the opposite extreme are those who insist that the body is nothing but an idea. Material substance apart from our idea of it does not exist; thinking substance, soul or spirit alone exists. This may exist after death. (Idealists)[2]

C. Others say man is a physical entity which functions in a certain way to produce the by-product called mind. The mind, soul or spirit cannot exist as an independent entity. As the liver secretes bile, the brain secretes thought. Nothing personal continues after death. (Epiphenomenalists)[3]

D. Actually we know nothing about either material or spiritual entities in themselves, another group argues, all we know are relationships. Man in relationship to all the complexities of this life cannot continue after death. (Pragmatists, John Dewey)[4]

E. Many contemporary theologians agree that the Bible does not speak of distinct material or spiritual entities in themselves. Rather, they say, the Bible teaches only about the whole man as he is morally and spiritually related to God. The whole man dies, and ceases to exist until the resurrection of the body. There is no intermediate state of a part of man. (Various schools of contemporary thought)[5]

F. Man is a complex creature of God composed not only of a physical body, but also of an immaterial self, soul or spirit. In the present life body and soul interact upon each other in such intricate ways that they are not easily distinguished. Nevertheless, the characteristics of the soul cannot be attributed to merely physical organism. They remain distinct, though interacting components. Death separates the soul from the body. Then the soul continues an incomplete, but conscious existence until the resurrection of the body and glorification of the whole man. (Orthodox Christians)[6]

II. *Problem*
Which understanding of man's nature best squares with the evidence of divine revelation? (To be answered in IV, only after examining the evidence in III)

III. *Procedure*
Seek the scriptural position on questions arising out of these alternative anthropologies.

A. Are there certain human characteristics which are less appropriately attributed to a material body than to a soul or spirit?

1. Can man know himself, consciously analyze his own thinking and thus transcend his own knowledge?

Ps. 4:4	*1 Cor. 11:28,31*	*Gal. 6:4*
1 Cor. 2:11	*2 Cor. 13:5*	*Summarize.*

2. Can man rule himself, consciously purpose to exercise his will in a certain way and thus transcend his own will?

Prov. 16:32   *Rom. 6:12*   *1 Cor. 9:25-27*
Prov. 25:28   *1 Cor. 7:37*   *Summarize.*

3. Is man morally responsible for his ethical judgments concerning what is right and wrong and for a clear conscience?

Isa. 5:20   *Rom. 14:12*   *1 Tim. 4:2*
Acts 23:1   *1 Tim. 1:5*   *Summarize.*
Acts 24:16

4. Can man fellowship with God?

Ex. 25:22   *2 Cor. 13:14*   *Summarize.*
1 Cor. 1:9   *1 Jn. 1:3*

5. In sum, man is characterized by the powers of self-transcendence, self-consciousness, self-determination, moral judgment, and communion with God. These qualities are not found in material things, the body, or the brain. "All materialism makes matter more than matter is." Matter cannot transcend itself, examine itself, have power over itself, judge between right and wrong, or pray to God. Do we not have in addition to the biblical evidence for man's physical being, biblical evidence for the existence of an actual, immaterial, intelligent, purposive, responsible self?

B. What is the relation of this immaterial self to the body?

1. What relationship do the following passages indicate?

2 Cor. 4:7,10   *2 Cor. 5:1-6*   *Heb. 13:3*
2 Cor. 4:16   *Phil. 1:24*

2. Does the body act upon or influence the immaterial self?

Mt. 26:41   *Eph. 5:29*
2 Cor. 12:7   *1 Pet. 2:11*

3. Does the immaterial self act upon the body?

Rom. 6:12-13,19   *1 Cor. 6:20*   *Jas. 3:2-3,6*
Rom. 12:1   *1 Cor. 9:27*   *Summarize B.*
Rom. 13:14

C. In spite of the intimate interaction of the inward and outward man, can the self exist after death?

Mt. 10:28	*Phil. 1:22*	*Rev. 6:9*
2 Cor. 5:6-8	*Heb. 12:23*	*Summarize.*

D. Write out and memorize Mt. 10:28.

IV. *Your Conclusion*

Evaluate the varied theories of man's nature and state your own conclusion on the subject.

V. *Significance*

A. What attitude should a Christian take toward the body (1 Tim. 4:1-5; Rom. 12:1-2; 1 Cor. 6:19-20)?

B. In a day of extreme attention to the care of the body is man in danger of neglecting the eternal well-being of his soul (1 Thess. 5:23)?

Notes

[1]Gustav A. Wetter, *Dialectical Materialism* (New York: Frederick A. Praeger, 1958), pp. 469-487.

[2]George Berkeley, *Principles of Human Knowledge* reprinted without abridgement in *The English Philosophers from Bacon to Mill,* ed. by Edwin A. Burtt (New York: Random House, 1939), pp. 507-579.

[3]T. H. Huxley, "Animal Automatism," selections from which are reprinted in *Body, Mind, and Death,* ed. by Antony Flew (New York: The Macmillan Co., 1964), pp. 196-205.

[4]John Dewey, *Experience and Nature* (LaSalle, Illinois: The Open Court Pub. Co., 1925); J. Oliver Buswell, Jr., *The Philosophies of F. R. Tennant and John Dewey* (New York: Philosophical Library, 1950), pp. 443-500.

[5]Oscar Cullmann, "Immortality or Resurrection?" *Christianity Today,* II (July 21, 1958), 3-6, and (August 18, 1958), 13-17.

[6]J. Oliver Buswell, Jr., *A Christian View of Being and Knowing* (Grand Rapids: Zondervan, 1960), pp. 126-160; Bernard Ramm, *Protestant Christian Evidences* (Chicago: Moody Press, 1954), pp. 58-70; Stuart C. Hackett, *The Resurrection of Theism* (Chicago: Moody Press, 1957), pp. 220-229.

11

How is finite, fallen man like God?

I. *Background*

Some measure the value of a human being by the rising cost of the body's chemical elements. In an industrial age others think men worth their salt only as tool-making animals. Marxists regard man important in so far as he may be used to establish a classless economic society. Others appear to hold that man's value depends upon his devotion to the scientific method of verification or a philosophical analysis of language.

But Christianity teaches that man is uniquely significant to the extent that he resembles God. It is the divine image and likeness that distinguishes man from everything else in creation. Christians have not always agreed, however, as to what that means. How is finite, fallen man like God?

A. The image of God, some say, is man's upright body. (Latter-day Saints)[1]

B. The image of God is man's capacity for moral action, which remains in spite of the fall into sin. Only the supernatural original righteousness was lost at the fall of man. (Roman Catholics)[2]

C. The image of God is (1) man's capacity for moral and spiritual action and (2) the proper use of that capacity. Both, however, were totally lost at the fall into sin. "Man who was little different from the angels is now little more than a brute." (Luther)[3]

D. The image of God is (1) man's capacity for moral and spiritual action and (2) the proper use of that capacity. At the fall into sin only the proper exercise of the capacity was totally lost, the capacity itself remains in a corrupted and depraved state. (Calvin)[4]

E. The image of God is not anything in fallen man's life; it is not like the imprint of a cookie cutter on a cookie. Rather, the image of God is a sheer reflection of God's character, like the reflection of the moon on the surface of a lake. Only when a man is properly related to God does he reflect the divine likeness. (Many contemporary theologians)[5]

F. The image of God is complex, involving: (1) man's dominion over the earth and the animals, (2) man's capacity for moral action, (3) man's proper use of that capacity, (4) a spiritual relationship to God. Since the fall into sin (1) man's dominion is disturbed by the curse on nature, (2) his ability to live righteously is corrupted, (3) consequently his righteousnesses are as filthy rags in God's sight, and (4) he is spiritually dead, separated from God, failing to reflect the divine likeness. (Evangelicals)[6]

II. *Problem*
Which view of God's image in man best accounts for all the scriptural teaching on the subject? (To be answered in IV,

only after examining all of the evidence in III)

III. *Procedure*

Answer questions arising out of these differing views after examining relevant Scripture.

A. Is man's likeness to God physical?

Jn. 4:24 with Lk. 24:39   *Deut. 4:15-16*

1 Tim. 1:17   *Isa. 40:18-25*   *Summarize.*

1 Tim. 6:16   *Rom. 1:23*

B. Why are male and female explicitly said to be created in the image of God (Gen. 1:27; 5:1-2)? God created the woman from the man to be his companion and helper. Is mankind created like God to commune with him and to share his purposes and work?

Gen. 2:18   *1 Cor. 11:3*   *1 Cor. 11:11-12*

Gen. 2:20   *1 Cor. 11:7-9*   *Summarize.*

C. Does the divine image in man include dominion over animals and nature?

Gen. 1:26   *Ps. 8:4-8*   *Heb. 2:6-8*

Gen. 1:28   *Rom. 8:18-23*   *Summarize.*

Gen. 9:1-2

D. Is fallen man still in the image of God (at least to some degree, or partially)?

Gen. 5:1,3   *1 Cor. 11:7*   *Summarize.*

Gen. 9:6   *Jas. 3:9*

E. Is the image of God in fallen man partially destroyed and in need of restoration?

Eph. 4:24   *2 Cor. 3:18*   *Summarize.*

Col. 3:10   *Rom. 8:29*

F. Does the renewed image of God include the use of man's capacity for knowledge of God and his will?

Col. 3:10

G. Does the renewed image of God include the use of man's capacity for a life of righteousness and holiness?

Eph. 4:24

H. Is the renewed image of God also a progressive reflection of a Christlike character when a man is properly related to God?

2 Cor. 3:18   *1 Cor. 15:49 and 1 Jn. 3:2*

Rom. 8:29   *Ps. 17:15*   *Summarize.*

I. Write out and memorize 2 Cor. 3:18.

IV. *Your Conclusion*

In your own words state what the Bible teaches about God's image in man, indicating why you believe as you do.

V. *Significance*

A. Is man's likeness to God any justification for use of images in worship? May pictures and statues be used for purposes of teaching?

B. If all men are to some extent in the image of God, how should all men be treated?

C. How does man's fundamental loneliness and restlessness relate to the loss of his moral likeness to God and his spiritual communion with God?

D. What does God's command to rule the earth have to do with the development of scientific knowledge?

Notes

[1] Joseph Smith, trans., *The Book of Mormon* (Salt Lake City, Utah: The Church of Jesus Christ of Latter-Day Saints, 1920), Ether 3:6-15, pp. 483-484.

[2] Charles Hodge, *Systematic Theology* (Grand Rapids: Wm. B. Eerdmans, 1946), II, pp. 103-106; Josef Neuner and Heinrich Roos, *The Teaching of the Catholic Church,* ed. by Karl Rahner (New York: The Mercier Press, 1967), pp. 127-129.

[3] Martin Luther, *Commentary on Genesis* excerpts from which are quoted in *A Compend of Luther's Theology,* ed. by Hugh Thomson Kerr (Philadelphia: The Westminster Press, 1943), pp. 79-83.

[4] John Calvin, *Institutes of the Christian Religion,* I, XV (Philadelphia: Presbyterian Board of Christian Education, n.d.), pp. 206-210.

[5] Paul Ramsey, *Basic Christian Ethics* (New York: Charles Scribner's Sons, 1950), pp. 249-284; David Cairns, *The Image of God in Man* (London: SCM Press, 1953), pp. 146-252.

[6] G. C. Berkouwer, *Man: The Image of God* (Grand Rapids: Wm. B. Eerdmans, 1962), pp. 1-363; J. Oliver Buswell, Jr., *A Systematic Theology of the Christian Religion,* I (Grand Rapids: Zondervan, 1962), pp. 231-254.

12

How sinful is man?

I. *Background*

As some look upon life the most important issues are the technological, the intellectual, the sensual, or the political. But Christians know that the most crucial of all are moral and spiritual. Out of the heart are the issues of life. Disastrously, however, man at heart and center is not right.

Although taboo for years, the word sin is coming back into the vocabulary of thinkers in many fields. Novelist James Jones, wounded in the battle for Guadalcanal, observes in *The Thin Red Line,* that "life for most people is nothing but a jungle . . . Morally, man is now the same in peace as he is in war. The only difference is that in peace the knives people stick in each other are only verbal." And William Golding wrote *Lord of the Flies* in "an attempt to trace the defects of society back to the defects of human nature." Golding explained, "We all saw . . . a lot in the war that can't be accounted for except on the basis of original evil." And the English philosopher C. E. M. Joad finally came to see that "evil is not merely a by-product of unfavorable circumstances; it is too widespread and too deep-seated to admit of any such explanation; so widespread, so deep-seated that one can only conclude that what the religions have always taught is true, that evil is endemic in the heart of man."[1] But not all have agreed with this analysis of man. What views have been held?

A. Human nature is originally good. Any evil in it results from the changes made upon it by external things. (Mencius, B.C. 372-289)[2]

B. Human nature is neither good nor bad; it is morally neutral, and can be influenced in either direction. (Naturalists)[3]

C. Any evil in human nature remains from a prior animal state which is being progressively overcome by the inevitable progress of evolution. In spite of any temporary setbacks, we have every reason to be optimistic about man's ability to build a utopian society. (Modernists)[4]

D. Modernists erred because they did not take the account of man's fall into sin seriously; Fundamentalists err in taking the story of the garden of Eden literally. The truth in the Genesis myth is that every man and woman inevitably falls into sin—the sin of claiming more for himself, his ideas and his interests than their objective importance would warrant. (Neo-orthodox theologians)[5]

E. As a result of the first parent's sin, man who was originally righteous, became inherently inclined to sin. Because all men are sinners inwardly, they commit outward acts of sin. Original sin affects every aspect of man's existence. It does not always appear evil; sin is worship and service (!) of the creature more than the Creator. (Evangelicals)[6]

II. *Problem*
Which view of man's inherent moral and spiritual condition is true? (To be answered in IV only after examining the evidence in III)

III. *Procedure*
Answer questions basic to these various doctrines of man and sin from your own study of relevant Scripture.

A. Is sin merely the result of an evil environment, or is it more fundamentally a condition of the heart or core of man's being?

Prov. 4:23	*Mk. 7:14-23*
Mt. 12:33-37	*Summarize.*

B. Is the human heart, (1) morally neutral, (2) inclined predominantly to love God and neighbor or (3) inclined predominantly to idolatry and selfishness (i.e. in a state of original sin)?

Gen. 6:5	*Jer. 17:9*	*Eph. 2:3*
Ps. 51:5	*Jn. 3:6*	*Eph. 4:18*
Isa. 48:8	*Rom. 7:18*	*Summarize.*
Isa. 64:6		

C. Does the sinfulness of man's heart affect every aspect of man's life?

1. The mind?

Rom. 8:7-8	*2 Cor. 4:4*	*1 Tim. 6:5*
1 Cor. 2:14	*Eph. 4:18*	*Tit. 1:15*

2. The will?

Prov. 1:25,30	*Ezek. 3:7*	*1 Pet. 4:2-3*
Isa. 30:9	*Rom. 6:16-17,20*	*2 Pet. 2:19*

3. The affections?

Jn. 3:19	*Col. 3:5,7*	*Summarize C.*
Eph. 2:3	*Tit. 3:3*	

D. Is man by himself able to change the sinful inclination of his heart?

Job 14:14	*Jn. 8:34*	*Rom. 7:14-25*

Jer. 13:23	*Rom. 5:6*	*Summarize.*
Jn. 6:44	*Rom. 6:16,20*	

E. How does man's sinful heart reveal itself in life?

1 Sam. 12:23	*Jn. 16:9*	*1 Jn. 3:4*
Prov. 14:21	*Rom. 1:21-32*	*Summarize.*
Prov. 24:9	*Gal. 5:19-21*	

F. Does sin always appear wicked to human observation? According to the following passages, what acts may be sinful?

Prov. 21:4c	*Mt. 23:23*	*Rom. 1:25*
Mt. 10:37	*Mt. 23:29*	*Jas. 4:17*
Mt. 23:14	*Lk. 18:9-14*	*Summarize.*
Mt. 23:15		

G. Are there any responsible human beings who are not sinners?

1 Kings 8:46	*Rom. 3:10-20,23*	*Summarize.*
Ps. 143:2	*1 Jn. 1:8*	

H. What are the effects of the entrance of sin into the human race?

Gen. 3:23	*Jn. 5:24*	*Eph. 4:18*
Gen. 3:14-19	*Rom. 5:15,17*	*Rom. 5:16,18*
Rom. 5:12-14	*Rom. 6:23*	*Summarize.*
1 Cor. 15:22		

I. Write out and memorize Rom. 1:25.

IV. *Your Conclusion*

Summarize in your own words the major elements in the biblical view of sin as you see it.

V. *Significance*

A. If mankind's great moral disease is not external, but internal, how should the external symptoms in our environment and culture be diagnosed and treated?

B. If man is sinful to the core and cannot alter his nature, what hope is there in this life and in the next?

Notes

[1] C. E. M. Joad, *God and Evil* (New York: Harper and Brothers, 1943), p. 20.

[2] Mencius, in Ch'u Chai with Winberg Chai, *The Story of Chinese Philosophy* (New York: Washington Square Press, 1961), pp. 53-60.

[3] Jean Jacques Rousseau, *The Social Contract and Discourses* (New York: E. P. Dutton, 1950), pp. 221-231.

[4] H. Shelton Smith, *Changing Conceptions of Original Sin* (New York: Charles Scribner's Sons, 1955), pp. 164-197.

[5] *Ibid.*, pp. 198-229; Reinhold Niebuhr, *The Nature and Destiny of Man*, I (New York: Charles Scribner's Sons, 1951), pp. 178-264.

[6] William T. Bruner, *Children of the Devil: A Fresh Investigation of the Fall of Man and Original Sin* (New York: Philosophical Library, 1966).

PART V
Christ for us

13

How could the changeless God become a man?

I. *Background*

The problem of change long perplexed the Greek philosophers. They wondered how that which *is* could become something it is not. For example, what about the philosopher's socks? If darned until every bit of yarn is replaced, are they the same socks? Can they remain what they were and become something else?

So the students of the Bible wondered how Christ could remain God (Jn. 1:1) and become something else, a baby. Some people felt the invisible God could never change into an actual man. Others acknowledge the true humanity of Christ, but they cannot believe he was truly the eternal second Person of the Trinity. But some still defend the actual deity as well as humanity.

A. There were those who claimed Jesus' life in a physical body of parts and passions could not have been real. It must have been a mirage, a dream, a mere appearance. God would be contaminated by partaking of human flesh. (Docetists)[1]

B. Others said the human body and soul were real, but the spirit was not that of a man. Christ's humanity was incomplete. The spirit was that of the eternal Logos. (Apollinarians)[2]

C. Jesus, the best of men, Socinus argued, was promoted or adopted to divine status at a certain point such as his baptism. Only after that could he in any sense be called divine. (Socinians, Unitarians)[3]

D. Jesus was more than a man, he was the first and highest created angel. Leaving that position behind he began his life as a mere man, and after his death was exalted to a higher creaturely status than before. Never is he Jehovah God, only God's highest representative. (Arians, Jehovah's Witnesses)[4]

E. Jesus was fully human, including a sinful nature. Even though Jesus sinned, he is the finest symbol of divine love ever revealed to man. (Reinhold Niebuhr)[5]

F. Jesus was fully human (including a sinful nature) but he did not sin. God acts in the world through him, but *incognito*. Unbelieving men could observe Jesus without seeing the eternal Logos (the Christ) in him. (Karl Barth)[6]

G. Jesus Christ was eternally the second Person of the Trinity, sharing all the divine attributes. In no respect were these taken from him at the incarnation. In becoming flesh he added to his divine characteristics all the essentially human attributes (These did not include either a sinful nature or actual sin; Adam was truly human before he fell into sin). The properties of the divine and human natures did not combine to form a third nature (Eutychians) nor form two separate persons (Nestorians). Jesus Christ, then, was one person with two natures, divine and human. (Orthodox Christians)[7]

II. *Problem*

Which of these beliefs best represent the various aspects of scriptural teaching about Christ? (To be answered in IV only after examining the evidence in III)

III. *Procedure*

Answer the questions arising out of the different views from your own study of relevant Scripture.

A. Did Jesus possess a real, physical body subject to birth, growth, hunger, thirst, fatigue and death?

Lk. 1:30,31	*Jn. 19:28*	*Lk. 23:46,52-55*
Lk. 2:7,11	*Jn. 4:6*	*Heb. 2:14*
Lk. 2:52	*Mk. 4:39*	*Summarize.*
Mt. 21:18		

B. Did Jesus also possess a real human spirit (a whole human nature, and not just the physical part)? Was Jesus fully human?

Lk. 23:46	*1 Cor. 15:21,47*	*Heb. 2:17*
Jn. 11:33	*1 Tim. 2:5*	*Summarize.*
Jn. 13:21		

C. Did Jesus become divine at his baptism or was he the Son of God from birth?

Mt. 1:23	*Lk. 1:35*	*Summarize.*
Mt. 2:2	*Lk. 2:11*	

D. Did Jesus ever sin?

Jn. 8:46	*1 Pet. 2:22*	*1 Jn. 3:5*
2 Cor. 5:21	*1 Pet. 3:18*	*Summarize.*

E. Did Jesus have a sinful nature?

Lk. 1:35	*Heb. 7:26*	*1 Pet. 1:19*
Jn. 10:11	*Heb. 9:14*	*Summarize.*
Jn. 17:16		

F. Was Jesus the highest of the angels or higher than the angels?

Heb. 1:4-5	*Heb. 1:8-13*	*Summarize.*

G. Was Jesus truly and fully God? (See also Study Guide 5

on Christ as a member of the Trinity.)

Mt. 1:23	*Rom. 9:5*	*1 Jn. 5:20*
Jn. 1:1	*Heb. 1:6*	*Summarize.*
Jn. 20:28		

H. Was Jesus' deity completely veiled in human flesh apart from faith or could unbelievers incur greater judgment because knowing him as God they inexcusably rejected his deity?

1 Tim. 3:16	*Heb. 1:1*	*Mk. 12:1-11*
Mk. 7:24	*Heb. 2:3-4*	*Summarize.*
Mk. 1:24,34	*Mt. 11:21-24*	

I. How then did the second Person of the eternal Godhead become incarnate? He did not cease to be deity (G.) or give up his divine powers (he could raise the dead, control nature and forgive sin). In entering the world as a human, did he then add or take on human characteristics and voluntarily choose to exercise his divine powers only intermittently and through a body in order to fulfill his redemptive mission? If so, he humbled or emptied himself not by being less than he eternally was, but in the way he used his divine capacities in order to save sinners.

Phil. 2:6-8	*Heb. 2:14-15,17*	*Summarize.*

J. Write out and memorize Col. 1:19.

IV. *Your Conclusion*
Explain in your own words how God became man, differentiating your view from others.

V. *Significance*
A. Was Jesus divine because he lived a perfect life or was he able to live a perfect life because he was divine?
B. If Jesus was not God could he forgive sin (Mk. 2:10)?
C. What practical difference does belief in Christ's deity make to your commitment to him as Lord of your life?

Notes

[1] H. R. Mackintosh, *The Doctrine of the Person of Jesus Christ* (Edinburgh: T. & T. Clark, 1912), pp. 383-385.

[2] *Ibid.,* pp. 196-201.

[3] *Ibid.,* pp. 245-246.

[4] *Ibid.,* pp. 175-195.

[5] Reinhold Niebuhr, *The Nature and Destiny of Man,* II (New York: Charles Scribner's Sons, 1951), pp. 73-74.

[6] Karl Barth, *Church Dogmatics* (Edinburgh: T. & T. Clark, 1956), I/2, pp. 147-159; I/1, pp. 184-212; D. M. Baillie, *God Was in Christ* (New York: Charles Scribner's Sons, 1948).

[7] G. C. Berkouwer, *The Person of Christ* (Grand Rapids: Wm. B. Eerdmans, 1954); Arthur W. Klem, "D. M. Baillie on the Person of Christ," *Bulletin of the Evangelical Theological Society,* VII (Spring 1964), pp. 45-52.

14

How shall we understand events in the earthly career of Christ?

I. *Background*

No mere philosophy of eternal truths, Christianity is the product of God's redemptive activity on earth. God came to visit us! Jesus displayed the unique glory of the Father (Jn. 1:18). Through Christ God was manifest in the flesh (1 Tim. 3:16).

In the life of Christ, how are the events most significant for Christian doctrine to be understood? Can Christ's virgin birth, miracles, death and resurrection be fully explained by naturalistic theories of history or science? On the other hand, are such occurrences totally removed from historical and scientific investigation taking place in some super-earthly realm?

A. Some believe only those acts of Christ which admit of a natural explanation and are similar to happenings in the lives of other men. Therefore they accept from the New Testament only those accounts of Christ's life which fit their modern scientific mentality. This they call the Jesus of history. Jesus may have been a marvelously good man and founder of one of the world's religions, but "We can now know almost nothing concerning the life and personality of Jesus." However there is no essential relationship between Jesus and faith in the Christ. (Bultmann)[1]

B. Others point out that what actually happened in the past is not limited to what can now be historically verified. Jesus' miracles, they insist, although not scientifically demonstrable, may have occurred. Whether they occurred or not is left up to the endless debates of technical specialists and held to be irrelevant to the Christian as such. What Christianity teaches, they say, is not science or history, but the *kerygma* (the gospel) and the meaning of history. Jesus may not have performed the miracles in fact, but we must accept his messiahship by faith. He may not have risen from the dead, but Christians believe he lives. To unbelieving "historians" and "scientists" Jesus appeared like an ordinary natural man. He was God incognito. Only when exercising faith in spite of evidence to the contrary, did men receive the Christian understanding of Jesus. What is important, for the faithful, is not facts about Christ, but theological meaning conveyed by Christ. (Neo-orthodox theologians)[2]

C. A third group maintains that since Jesus is truly human and truly divine, some aspects of his earthly career are open to historical investigation and some are not. Insofar as his miracles were visible events in the physical world, they were subject to eyewitness confirmation. To the extent that those same phenomena were produced by the power of the invisible God, they could not be checked by the five senses (seeing, hearing, touching, tasting, smelling). The man who was born blind suddenly could see! That much could be observed. Jesus put clay and saliva upon his eyes. That too could be checked, although it did not uniformly enable the blind to see. But the power of the invisible God could not be so tested; it was however, acknowledged as a result of the "signs" attesting the fact that he was the Son of the living God. In spite of modern prejudgment to contrary, these visible events did take place, and they function most relevantly as "signs" authenticating the supreme Messenger of God. Faith in the meaning of Christ's earthly career is founded on the observable facts of that career. (Orthodox Christians)[3]

II. *Problem*
Which of the stated positions best reflects the view of the New Testament writers concerning Jesus' incarnate life? (To be answered in IV only after examining the evidence in III)

III. *Procedure*
Examine scriptural events in Christ's life to determine which understanding of them best fits the evidence.

A. Did Mary, Matthew, and Luke the physician establish that neither Joseph nor any other man contributed to the conception of Jesus?

Mt. 1:18	*Mt. 1:25*	*Lk. 1:34*
Mt. 1:23	*Lk. 1:27*	*Summarize.*

B. Did God reveal that the conception of Jesus was by the power of the invisible Holy Spirit?

Mt. 1:18	*Lk. 1:35*
Mt. 1:20	*Summarize.*

C. Considering the biblical data in both A. and B., is the modernist, neo-orthodox or evangelical view supported? Was the virgin birth in its entirety a matter of revelation from God? Was it in its entirety a matter of fact subject to investigation? Or were history and revelation combined? Would the theological point (B.) be as meaningful if the fact in A. were not confirmed?

D. Were unbelievers as well as Christ's disciples able to

confirm the historical fact of Jesus' death on the cross?

Mk. 15:39   Jn. 19:31-34

Mk. 15:43-45   *Summarize.*

E. From what source did the apostles learn the meaning of his death—"for our sins"? Could this have been established by observation, or was revelation necessary?

Gal. 1:11-12   Eph. 3:3

1 Cor. 15:3   *Summarize.*

F. Considering the biblical data in both D. and E. is Jesus' death in its Christian understanding a matter of mere investigation, mere revelation, or both? Could Christians hold the significance of Christ's death if the fact had not occurred?

G. Was Christ's resurrection subject to verification by the senses of sight, hearing and touch?

Jn. 20:27   Lk. 24:39-43   *Summarize.*

How many recorded confirmations of Jesus' risen body were made?

1 Cor. 15:5-8   Lk. 24   Jn. 20-21

H. What meaning did revelation attach to the event of Christ's resurrection from the grave?

Acts 17:30-31   Acts 10:43   Eph. 1:20-22

Acts 10:40-42   Rom. 4:25   *Summarize.*

Was the meaning of the resurrection valid if the fact did not occur?

1 Cor. 15:13-19

I. Write out and memorize 1 Cor. 15:3-4.

V. *Your Conclusion*

In your own words explain your understanding of events in the life of Christ regarding their actuality, their meaning and the relation between the two.

VI. *Significance*

A. Evaluate the statements of Emil Brunner: "Whether the biblical writers and the various facts which they record, are credible, has nothing whatever to do with 'faith' in the biblical sense" (*Revelation and Reason,* p. 176). "In faith we are not concerned with the Jesus of history, as historical science sees him, but with the Jesus Christ of personal testimony .... Faith presupposes, as a matter of course, *a priori,* that the Jesus of history is not the same as the Christ of faith" (*The Mediator,* p. 159, 184).

B. Why did Jesus live in literal history as a man (Heb. 2:14-18; 4:15-16)?

Notes

[1] Rudolph Bultmann, *Jesus and the Word* (New York: Charles Scribner's Sons, 1958), p. 8; Robert D. Knudsen, "Rudolph Bultmann," *Creative Minds in Contemporary Theology*, ed. by Philip Edgecomb Hughes (Grand Rapids: Wm. B. Eerdmans, 1966), pp. 131-162.

[2] Emil Brunner, *The Mediator* (Philadelphia: The Westminster Press, 1947), pp. 153-198, 322-327, 355-376, and 573-584; Karl Barth, *Church Dogmatics* (Edinburgh: T. & T. Clark, 1956), I/2, pp. 122-202.

[3] Carl F. H. Henry, ed., *Jesus of Nazareth: Saviour and Lord* (Grand Rapids: Wm. B. Eerdmans, 1966); Daniel P. Fuller, *Easter Faith and History* (Grand Rapids: Wm. B. Eerdmans, 1965); George Ladd, *Jesus Christ and History* (Chicago: Inter-Varsity Press, 1963).

15

How did Christ atone for man's sin?

I. *Background*

Because man's deepest problem is a moral and spiritual "disease" (Study Guide 12), his fundamental need lies in a moral and spiritual "cure." The plight of man stems from the very core of his being and affects every part. Therefore the cure cannot be found in any sinner or any sinner's program or organization. It must come from beyond the contaminated race. The hope of man is not in his limited and inadequate quest for God, but in God's redemptive provision for man. Christianity's distinctive claim is that the God-man, Jesus Christ, came to make available the complete cure for man's otherwise incurable malady.

But people have pictured Christ's saving activity very differently. Different diagnoses of the disease determine the extent of treatment needed. Some take one aspect of biblical teaching and make it the whole.

A. The only change necessary is in man's own repentance and self-corrected conduct. Jesus' death simply provides an *example* of unselfish martyrdom. If men would repent and follow his example, their problems would be solved. (Socinus and Unitarians)[1]

B. Jesus' death is not merely the noble example of a man but a moving expression of divine grace. While a mere human example is insufficient, the *moral influence* exerted convinces sinners of God's love and dissipates their enmity to God. (Bushnell, Schleiermacher, many liberals)[2]

C. Man needs more than an example or influence; he needs a direct act of God to deliver him from bondage to sin. Christ's atonement is pictured as a dramatic triumph over man's greatest enemies: sin and death, the law and Satan. Christ's ransom *redeems* men from the slave market of sin, liberating them from its power. (Aulén, "biblical" theologians)[3]

D. Sinners need deliverance not only from the power of sin, but also from its guilt. Christ's death provides satisfaction of God's holy law and *propitiates* his righteous wrath so that the believer will be pardoned all his sin and will not again come under condemnation. (Some fundamentalists)[4]

E. Man needs new spiritual life before he can fellowship with God. On the ground of Christ's atonement the believer is mystically identified with Christ, new life is imparted, and fellowship with God restored. The atonement primarily *reconciles* men to God. (Neo-orthodox theologians)[5]

F. Of course Christ's life and death exemplified love and exerted an influence for good. But Christ's atonement is far more profound than allowed by the example and influence theories. In addition Christ's death provided: (1) for the sinner's guilt a sinless substitutionary sacrifice which satisfies divine justice, (2) for the sinner's enslavement, an inestimably precious ransom which dramatically delivers from sin's "slave market," and (3) for the sinner's estrangement from God a complete reconciliation which restores full fellowship and inheritance privileges in the divine household. (Evangelicals, some fundamentalists)[6]

II. *Problem*
Which of the above views best represents biblical teaching? (To be answered in IV only after examining the evidence)

III. *Procedure*
Answer questions arising out of the different views from the Bible itself.
    A. In what ways was Jesus' death an example?

Eph. 5:2	*Heb. 12:1-3*	*1 Pet. 4:1-2*
Phil. 2:3-8	*1 Pet. 2:21-23*	*Summarize.*

    B. Did Jesus' death exercise an influence for good upon others?

Lk. 23:42,47	*Eph. 5:2*
2 Cor. 5:14	*Summarize.*

    C. Did Jesus' death provide a ransom paid to redeem men from the bondage of sin and set them free?

Isa. 61:1	*Rom. 8:2*	*1 Pet. 1:18*
Mk. 10:45 (Mt. 20:28)	*Eph. 1:7*	*Rev. 5:9*
Jn. 8:36	*Tit. 2:14*	*Summarize.*

    D. In dying did Jesus propitiate (appease) God's righteous wrath by bearing divine judgment as a substitute for sinners?

Isa. 53:5-6	*Eph. 5:2*	*1 Jn. 4:10*
Rom. 3:25	*Heb. 9:28*	*Rev. 1:5*
2 Cor. 5:21	*1 Pet. 3:18*	*Summarize.*
Gal. 1:4	*1 Jn. 2:2*	

    E. Did Christ's atonement provide the basis for the reconciliation of estranged sinners to divine fellowship?

Rom. 5:10-11	*Eph. 2:12-16*	*Summarize.*
2 Cor. 5:18-20	*Col. 1:20-22*	

F. Write out and memorize 2 Cor. 5:21.

IV. *Your Conclusion*

Sum up the teaching of Scripture as you see it on the way in which Christ atoned for man's sin.

V. *Significance*

A. Christians sometimes fail to enjoy freedom from the dominion of sin, feelings of guilt and estrangement from God. Does it follow that Christ's provision for redemption, justification and reconciliation was not completed once-for-all?

B. Karl Barth, in opposition to the subjectivism of religious liberalism stresses the objective effects of Christ's atonement. Christ's death, Barth teaches, actually achieved justification, conversion and sanctification for all men. Barth does not make the classical distinction between Christ's objective provision of atonement and the individual's personal appropriation of its benefits. According to Barth, "the destroying and the renewing (conversion) have taken place for all men. . . . Unbelief has become an objective, real and ontological impossibility and faith an objective, real and ontological necessity for all men and for every man" (*Church Dogmatics* IV, 1, p. 747). Evaluate Barth's tendency toward universalism. Did Christ die for all? Are all then justified? Why?

C. Evaluate the statement: "It makes no difference what view of Christ's atonement you hold theologically so long as you have faith in Jesus."

Notes

[1] Robert H. Culpepper, *Interpreting the Atonement* (Grand Rapids: Wm. B. Eerdmans, 1966), pp. 103-105.

[2] *Ibid.*, pp. 113-115.

[3] Gustav Aulén, *Christus Victor* (London: SPCK, 1953).

[4] Archibald Alexander Hodge, *The Atonement* (Grand Rapids: Wm. B. Eerdmans, 1953).

[5] Emil Brunner, *Truth As Encounter* (Philadelphia: The Westminster Press, 1964), pp. 153-160; Karl Barth, *Church Dogmatics* (Edinburgh: T. & T. Clark, 1956), IV/1, p. 22.

[6] Leon Morris, *The Cross in the New Testament* (Grand Rapids: Wm. B. Eerdmans, 1965); Roger Nicole, "The Nature of Redemption," *Christian Faith and Modern Theology*, ed. by Carl F. H. Henry (New York: Channel Press, 1964), pp. 193-222.

PART VI

the Holy Spirit in us

16

How does the Holy Spirit help a person become a Christian?

I. *Background*

Salvation involves not only Jesus Christ's objective provision, but also a person's subjective appropriation. How does a sinner come to a realization of divine pardon, ransom and reconciliation?

Does an individual start the Christian life without any help from God the Holy Spirit? Or, is the Spirit's activity as necessary as Christ's? If the Holy Spirit dispenses the saving grace of God, how does he achieve this?

A. Some think salvation is all of man. Created in the divine image, men have not been debilitated by sin. What God commands, man is able to perform. If the Holy Spirit in any way is said to help, it is indirectly through the conscience. Man has the intelligence to determine God's will and the ability to do what he judges to be right. (Pelagians, Unitarians, modernists)[1]

B. Others, eliminating human responsibility, have held that salvation is all of God. What God commands man cannot perform. Sinners, totally depraved cannot understand the gospel if they would, and they would not believe if they could "see" it. Whom he pleases the Holy Spirit saves apart from any human agency. If God wants to save others he will do so apart from any human missionary endeavor. (Fatalists, hyper-Calvinists)[2]

C. A third group maintains that in salvation a man takes the initiative and then the Holy Spirit begins to help. In spite of the fall, through grace given to all men a sinner can understand and receive the gospel persuasively presented by Christian servants. As a result of a sinner's repentant-faith (conversion), the Holy Spirit regenerates him and enables him to live the Christian life. Growth in grace finds its ultimate explanation in the work of the Holy Spirit and its proximate explanation in the efforts of men. After the beginning of salvation a man is never more free than when filled with the Holy Spirit. (Semi-Pelagians, Arminians)[3]

D. A fourth group believes that the Holy Spirit takes the initiative in "calling" sinners to Christ through a verbal presentation of the gospel by Christian servants. As a result of the Spirit's regeneration the individual expresses the new life first in repentant-faith (conversion). Thus at the beginning of the Christian life as well as during its continuation the ultimate explanation is the action of the Holy Spirit and the proximate explanation is man's faith and yieldedness. At the beginning, as well as during the Christian life, a man is never more free than when under the influence of the Holy Spirit. (Calvinists)[4]

II. *Problem*
Which view best correlates biblical teaching on the origin of

the Christian life? (To be answered in IV only after examining the evidence in III)

III. *Procedure*
Answer questions arising out of these differences of opinion from your own examination of scriptural data.

A. Is salvation possible for the best of sinful men apart from the Spirit's gift of God's grace?

Rom. 3:10,20,23	*Gal. 3:21*	*Tit. 3:5-7*
Rom. 10:1-3	*Eph. 2:8-9*	*Summarize.*
Gal. 2:16		

B. Does God save people apart from human witnesses to the gospel? Or, while the Holy Spirit alone can save a man, has the Holy Spirit chosen never to save a man without some human activity?

Acts 1:8	*1 Cor. 3:9*	*2 Cor. 3:1-8*
Rom. 10:13-15	*1 Cor. 15:34*	*Summarize.*

C. Is regeneration, the imparting of a new spiritual life and nature, the work of the Holy Spirit alone?

Jn. 1:13	*Col. 2:13*	*Jas. 1:18*
Jn. 3:3-8	*Tit. 3:5-6*	*Summarize.*
Eph. 2:1		

D. Is conversion, the initial act of consciously turning from sin to Christ in repentant faith, an act of the sinner alone? Or is conversion an act of the sinner with the help of the Holy Spirit's conviction of sin, "call," illumination and power?

Jn. 16:8-9	*2 Thess. 2:13-14*	*1 Cor. 2:10-14*
Acts 11:18	*2 Tim. 1:9*	*2 Cor. 4:3-6*
2 Tim. 2:25	*Heb. 9:15*	*Acts 16:14*
1 Cor. 1:9	*1 Pet. 2:9*	*Summarize.*
1 Cor. 1:23-24	*1 Cor. 2:4-5*	

E. As an individual begins the Christian life, is the initiative with God or the sinner? The Calvinist thinks the passages in D. place the initiative with God. The Arminian thinks the following passages place the initiative with the sinner. What do you understand these passages to teach in relation to those in D.?

Mk. 1:15	*Acts 8:37*	*Rom. 1:16*
Jn. 1:12	*Acts 10:43*	*Rom. 3:22*
Jn. 3:15-18,36	*Acts 13:39*	*Rom. 10:13*
Jn. 5:24	*Acts 16:31*	*Summarize.*
Acts 2:38		

F. If one permanently rejects the Spirit's witness to the truth of the gospel of Christ, does he call God a liar and blaspheme the Spirit by ascribing his work to Satan or evil spirits? Does such a rejection of the salvation which the Father plans, the Son provides and the Spirit applies, leave a person any hope of divine forgiveness?

Mk. 3:20-30	*Heb. 6:4-8*	*1 Jn. 5:16-17 (cf. 2:19,*
Lk. 11:15-20	*Heb. 10:26-29*	*22; 4:2-3; 5:1,5,10)*
Mt. 12:24,31-37	*1 Jn. 5:14-15*	*Summarize.*

G. Write out and memorize Jn. 16:8-9.

IV. *Your Conclusion*

In your own words explain the relation between the redemptive work of the Spirit and the responsible action of the individual who begins the Christian life. (Compare Study Guide 6.)

V. *Significance*

A. On your view of the Spirit's work in relation to an individual's conversion, is it meaningful to pray for the effectiveness of evangelistic efforts?

B. Should one who sincerely trusts Christ have doubts about being among God's elect? (Rom. 8:15-17; Gal. 4:6-7)

C. Need any Christian fear committing the unforgivable sin? Is that to be identified with the "ups and downs" of the Christian life or with a final repudiation of Christ as revealed in Spirit-illumined Scripture?

Notes

[1] J. N. D. Kelly, *Early Christian Doctrines* (New York: Harper & Brothers, 1958), pp. 357-361.

[2] Peter Toon, *The Emergence of Hyper-Calvinism in English Nonconformity 1689-1765* (London: The Olive Tree, 1967).

[3] H. Orton Wiley, *Christian Theology*, II (Kansas City: Beacon Hill Press, 1959), pp. 303-378.

[4] Abraham Kuyper, *The Work of the Holy Spirit* (Grand Rapids: Wm. B. Eerdmans, 1956), pp. 203-427; James I. Packer, *Evangelism and the Sovereignty of God* (Chicago: Inter-Varsity Press, 1961).

17

Can a Spirit-led
  Christian
  be holy?

I. *Background*

The New Testament boldly does what we hesitate to do. It calls all believers sanctified ones, "saints." Spirit-imparted life is separated from sin and consecrated to God. But to what extent? How fully can a Christian expect to overcome the effects of sin (Study Guide 12) and reorder his life in the image of God (Study Guide 11)?

As means to sanctification, Christians agree, the Holy Spirit employs diligent Bible study, sincere prayer, faithful churchmanship and dedicated witness to the world. But on the nature of sanctification Christians differ. What does sanctification mean?

A. Some think the life of the sanctified is not necessarily different from that of a non-Christian. Sanctification, like justification, is not experiential but formal. Regardless of the Christian's state, his standing before God is reckoned righteous. Identified with the crucified and risen Christ the believer is considered as perfectly sanctified as Christ. (This view by itself may appear in any branch of the church among anti-nomians or libertines.)[1]

B. Others identify the Christian life with legalistic human striving. Apart from any assistance of the Holy Spirit a person must suppress his evil desires and try to obey God's law. Motivated not by love but necessity, a person is sanctified to the extent that he has kept the commandments. (Legalists and moralists in many groups)[2]

C. A third position maintains that the Christian may achieve a state of perfection in this life. Subsequent to conversion a believer receives from the Holy Spirit a new crisis experience. Instantaneously the old nature is eradicated and perfect freedom from sin is enjoyed. The sanctified enjoy perfect love and complete freedom from fear. They do not commit any known sin. Some victorious life movements claim as well a state of complete freedom from temptation. (Wesley, holiness and some victorious life advocates)[3]

D. Although the believer's sanctification is perfect in Christ positionally, it is not perfect in this life experientially. Acceptance of Jesus Christ as Savior and Lord does not eradicate the tendency to worship and serve the creation more than the Creator. In many ways and at different times a believer yields to temptation. But sin does not have dominion over him. He has the God-given ability not to sin. By grace he can effectively counteract his own inner tendency to idolatry and selfishness. The battle to love God above all else and one's neighbor as oneself is never finished in this life. But the objective of nothing less than Christlike holy love motivates the Christian to employ every available resource in the progressive development of holiness in character and conduct. (Orthodox and evangelical theologians)[4]

II. *Problem*

Which view most accurately summarizes scriptural teaching on sanctification? (To be answered in IV only after examining the evidence in III)

III. *Procedure*

From the study of relevant Scripture seek the answer to questions arising out of the different concepts of the Christian life.

    A. Can the Christian united by faith to the risen Christ be considered completely sanctified in a positional sense?

Acts 20:32	*1 Cor. 6:11*	*Heb. 13:12*
Acts 26:18	*Heb. 10:10*	*Summarize.*
1 Cor. 1:2,30	*Heb. 10:29*	

    B. Apart from the help of the Holy Spirit, is the best human endeavor to keep God's commandments sufficient to fulfill the biblical standards of sanctification in the experience of a believer? (Is this because of imperfection in God's law or weakness in man's sinful nature?)

Rom. 7:7,12,14	*Gal. 2:21–3:3*	*Summarize.*
Rom. 7:5,13,18	*Gal. 3:21*	

    C. Is perfection in this life the Christian ideal?

Mt. 5:48	*Col. 1:28*	*Summarize.*
Rom. 8:29	*1 Pet. 1:15-16*	

    D. What are the biblical characteristics of perfection? Which quality is preeminent? Can any compromise of these standards be justifiably called sinless perfection?

2 Cor. 7:1	*1 Thess. 3:13*	*1 Cor. 13:1-3*
Eph. 1:4	*1 Thess. 4:3,7*	*Col. 3:14*
Eph. 4:24	*1 Thess. 5:23*	*1 Pet. 4:8*
Phil. 2:15	*Mt. 22:37-40*	*Summarize.*
Col. 3:10		

    E. Is perfection in this life possible?

Phil. 3:12-14	*1 Jn. 1:8,10*
1 Jn. 1:5-6	*Summarize.*

F. If perfection is impossible, does that give Christians license to persist in sin? Does the liberty of the Spirit, or of love, result in lawlessness?

Jn. 14:23-24	*Rom. 6:22*	*1 Jn. 3:9-10*
Jn. 15:14	*Rom. 8:2-4*	*1 Jn. 5:3-4,18*
Rom. 6:1-4	*Rom. 13:8-10*	*Summarize.*
Rom. 6:12-18		

G. Is the fleshly inclination eradicated in this life?

Rom. 8:11	*1 Jn. 3:2*
Rom. 8:20-23	*Summarize.*

H. Can a Christian expect to attain a level of victorious living in which he is never tempted?

Jn. 15:19-20	*Jn. 17:15-19*	*2 Cor. 4:8-11*
Jn. 16:1-4	*1 Cor. 10:1-12*	*Summarize.*
Jn. 16:33		

I. In the face of temptation, is the Spirit-filled Christian able not to yield (sin)?

1 Cor. 10:13	*2 Cor. 4:7,16*	*1 Jn. 4:4*
2 Cor. 2:14-16	*Eph. 5:18*	*1 Jn. 5:3-6*
2 Cor. 3:5	*Phil. 2:12-13*	*Summarize.*

J. Write out and memorize Gal. 5:22-23.

IV. *Your Conclusion*

In your own words explain the ideal of the Christian life and the possibility of its realization by the power of the Holy Spirit.

V. *Significance*

A. When a Christian does sin, can this change the fact of his regeneration and conversion (Study Guide 16)? What should a Christian do when he sins (1 Jn. 1:9; 2:1)?

B. In our technological culture how can a Christian's possessions be regarded holy (1 Tim. 4:3-5)?

C. According to the example of Christ, does the life of separation from sin and consecration to God mean isolation from sinners (Mt. 9:9-13)?

Notes

[1] Archibald Alexander Hodge, *Outlines of Theology* (Grand Rapids: Wm. B. Eerdmans, 1949), p. 526.

[2] *Ibid.,* pp. 527-541.

[3] H. Orton Wiley, *Christian Theology,* II (Kansas City: Beacon Hill Press, 1952), pp. 440-517.

[4] K. F. W. Prior, *The Way of Holiness* (Chicago: Inter-Varsity Press, 1967); B. B. Warfield, *Perfectionism,* 2 vols. (New York: Oxford University Press, 1931); Horatius Bonar, *God's Way of Holiness* (Chicago: Moody Press, n. d.).

18

Does love alone make an act good?

I. *Background*

Under the pseudonym of Hopalong Hippy a twenty-five year old man told a writer, "A hippy can be anybody, regardless of hair style, or color, or creed, or country of origin, if they express and try to live the Love Ethic.

"The Love Ethic is as basic as the Ten Commandments. What is it? Love thy neighbor; do unto others; be good to other people, be good to yourself, don't do anything to hurt anyone else."[1]

The supreme importance of doing good out of love is not often challenged. Problems arise, however, when we try to determine in some detail what is good for ourselves and others. How can we tell whether a given course of action is good for a given person at a given time? What makes a good work *good*?

A. There are those who identify the good with the individual's enjoyment. If a person does not like to do something, it is not necessary for him. Good works are relative to emotional tastes. (Egoistic hedonists)[2]

B. Others, reacting against the apparent selfishness of the first view, identify good works with actions which contribute to the greatest amount of enjoyment for the greatest number of people. The good is relative to the changing pleasure of the majority. (Altruistic hedonists, Utilitarians)[3]

C. Popular also is the position that classifies as good any action which gets the desired results. There is little agreement on the kind of results which are desirable in any given problem. And what "works" for one may not for another. (Pragmatists)[4]

D. In contrast to the relativism of the previous views some defend an objective and fixed standard of right and wrong in the Ten Commandments as given to Moses (Ex. 20). Although Moses' ceremonial laws are no longer binding upon the church and his civil laws are no longer binding upon the state, his moral law remains normative for all men. (Reformed theologians and others)[5]

E. Impressed with the rigidity of the moral law and with the difficulty of applying it in complex situations, another group appeals to no law but love. Any act is good if motivated by love for God and man, and evil if not so motivated. (*Agape* ethics appear in movements of varied kinds, for example in the new morality.)[6]

F. Joining opposition to the law as a rule of life in our dispensation, some charge Reformed Christians with legalism and emphasize the freedom of the Holy Spirit. What the Spirit leads a person to do in a given situation is good. Any act contrary to the Spirit's direction is evil. (Some dispensationalists)[7]

G. One further position regards as good any act of a Christian motivated by love for God and man, energized by the power of the Holy Spirit and consistent with the scriptural teaching on the Christian life. Most explicitly found in the practical portions of the New Testament, the biblical exhortations repeat nine of the Ten Commandments (The fourth is omitted). But recognition of God's expressed will does not involve legalism when there is dependence on the Spirit rather than the flesh. Difficulties of applying these guidelines for good works do not render them valueless. Divine love has been shed abroad in our hearts not to destroy divine commands, but to fulfill them. Jesus Christ exemplified the possibility of carrying out the will of God, out of a heart of love and by the power of the Holy Spirit. (Some evangelicals)[8]

II. *Problem*
Which of the explanations of good works should a Christian hold? (To be answered in IV only after examining the evidence in III)

III. *Procedure*
Questions arising out of the alternatives are to be answered from your own study of Scripture.

A. How important are good works to a Christian?

Mt. 7:24-27	*Tit. 1:16*	*Tit. 3:5,8,14*
Eph. 2:10	*Tit. 2:7*	*Summarize.*
Eph. 5:3-6	*Tit. 2:10,12,14*	

B. Is any act which gives the doer pleasure necessarily good?

Rom. 13:13-14	*2 Tim. 3:2-4*	*1 Pet. 2:11-12*
Gal. 5:17-24	*Tit. 2:11-12; 3:3*	*1 Pet. 4:2*
1 Tim. 5:6	*Heb. 11:25*	*Summarize.*

C. Is an act which increases the pleasure of a majority necessarily good?

Gen. 6:11-12	*Acts 4:18-19*	*Rom. 12:1-2*
Ps. 33:13-19	*Acts 21:34,36*	*1 Pet. 4:3-6*
Mt. 27:20-24	*Acts 25:24*	*Summarize.*

D. Is an act necessarily good if it produces the desired results?

Gen. 37:26-28	*Ps. 37:35-36*	*2 Sam. 11:2-5,14-15,27*
Rom. 3:8	*Mt. 7:16-20,22-23*	*Summarize.*

E. Is an act good if it allegedly springs from love but is contrary to divine exhortation and example? Is love, apart from relevant Scripture, a sufficient standard of conduct?

Jn. 12:25	*1 Jn. 2:5; 3:16; 5:3*	*Eph. 5:1-2*
Jn. 14:15	*2 Jn. 6*	*Phil. 1:9*
Jn. 15:10	*Lk. 6:27-35*	*Summarize.*

F. Is an act good if a believer feels led of the Holy Spirit to conduct contrary to scriptural teaching?

Jn. 8:32,36	*Gal. 5:1,13-24*	*1 Jn. 4:1-3*
1 Cor. 8:9	*1 Pet. 2:16*	*Summarize.*
1 Cor. 9:19	*2 Pet. 2:19*	

G. Is an act of a Christian good in the sight of God (apart from considerations of pleasure or result) if done according to God's scripturally revealed will, out of a heart of love, and in the power of the Holy Spirit?

Rom. 14:17-18	*Eph. 2:18-22*	*Col. 3:14,16-17*
Rom. 15:4-6	*Eph. 3:10,13-18*	*2 Tim. 3:16-17*
1 Cor. 10:1-11	*Eph. 4:13-15*	*2 Pet. 1:19*
1 Cor. 10:23–11:1	*Eph. 5:17-20*	*Summarize.*
2 Cor. 6:4-8		

H. For more specific principles of Christian conduct, you may choose to list, with the help of a concordance or topical index, biblical teaching on husbands and wives, parents and children, employers and employees, citizens and rulers, and so forth.

I. Write out and memorize Rom. 8:3-4.

IV. *Your Conclusion*

In your own words explain how you understand good works to be distinguished from evil or sinful works. (Compare Study Guide 12.)

V. *Significance*

A. In seeking the will of God in a given problem, what place does the Bible have?

B. Can a Christian acknowledge performance of a good work without pharisaic pride or morbid self-depreciation? Explain.

C. How can you exercise your Christian liberty and at the same time avoid license and lawlessness?

Notes

[1] Bernard Kelly, "What A Hippy Is," *Empire Magazine* (December 3, 1967), p. 10.

[2] Carl F. H. Henry, *Christian Personal Ethics* (Grand Rapids: Wm. B. Eerdmans, 1957), pp. 30-37.

[3] *Ibid.*, pp. 37-50.

[4] *Ibid.*, pp. 87-89.

[5] Charles Hodge, *Systematic Theology*, III (Grand Rapids: Wm. B. Eerdmans, 1946), pp. 259-465.

[6] Joseph Fletcher, *Moral Responsibility: Situation Ethics at Work* (Philadelphia: The Westminster Press, 1967).

[7] Lewis Sperry Chafer, *Systematic Theology* (Dallas: Dallas Seminary Press, 1948), III, 76-86, 342-345; IV, 154-251; VII, 225-226.

[8] Carl F. H. Henry, *op. cit.*, pp. 172-458.

PART VII
the church in the world

19

What is the Christian church?

I. *Background*

Christians are erecting impressive places of worship in unprecedented numbers. As a result concepts of the church often suffer from an edifice complex. Never in the Bible does the word church denote a cathedral or a chapel.

The church is not made up of bricks, but of people. Not all people, however, are members of the church. It does not include everyone uncommitted to a non-Christian religion. Neither does it involve everyone born in a "Christian" country.

Who belongs to the Christian church? Three major answers are given.

A. Some think that only those who enroll in a certain institutional church are in Christ's church. The prime example is traditional Roman Catholicism which taught that there could be no salvation outside its organization headed by the Pope. Similarly exclusive attitudes may develop in any of the forms of church organization, including nondenominational and interdenominational ones. Four major types of church government may be noted:

1. The institutional church is governed by a hierarchy of pastors under one visible head on earth, the Pope. (Roman Catholicism)[1]

2. The institutional church is governed by bishops and pastors who can trace their ordinational succession back to the first century apostles. (Anglican and Episcopalian)[2]

3. The institutional church is governed by sessions, presbyteries, synods and assemblies representing the members. (Lutherans and Presbyterians)[3]

4. The institutional church is governed by the vote of the membership itself. No higher authority on earth is recognized. Pastors are distinguished from others only in their distinctive function. (Baptists and other congregationally governed groups)[4]

B. Some, reacting against corruptions of doctrine or practice in institutional churches have defined the church apart from any necessary organizational relationship. The true members of Christ's church are those who through faith have a vital relationship with the living Christ himself. Three varieties of this spiritual church may be held:

1. Those believers who have genuine personal fellowship (Emil Brunner)[5]

2. All believers on earth at any one time (the universal church)[6]

3. All believers in heaven and earth from all times or since Pentecost (the invisible church)[7]

C. A third position combines both the spiritual and the institutional aspects in a normal church. Like the body and soul, both must be kept together. The institutional form without the vital relationship to Christ by faith is dead. The spiritual life without the institutional order is ineffective in this world. So believers participate in institutional churches. Temporary exceptions due to circumstances beyond human knowledge or control must be admitted. But so far as humanly possible every believer in the Lord joins an organized Christian church, and every member of a church is related to the Lord Jesus Christ by faith. (Many recent thinkers)[8]

II. *Problem*
Is the Christian church essentially institutional, or spiritual, or both? Which is the biblical view? (To be answered in IV only after examining the evidence in III)

III. *Procedure*
Answer questions arising out of the various positions.
   A. Is the church composed of people inwardly responsive to the triune God's salvation (the Father's call, the Son's redemption and the Spirit's presence)?
   1. Is the church made up of those who respond to the Father's call (summons) out of an unbelieving world?

1 Cor. 1:2,9	*2 Thess. 2:1,13-14*	*1 Pet. 5:10-13*
Eph. 4:4-6	*2 Tim. 1:9*	*Summarize.*

   2. Is an inner acceptance of God the Son as Saviour and Lord (head of the body) necessary to being part of that body (the church)?

Acts 2:36,41	*Eph. 1:1,15*	*Col. 1:3-4*
1 Cor. 1:2	*Eph. 2:8-22*	*Col. 1:18-23*
1 Cor. 3:5-10	*Eph. 3:6*	*Summarize.*

   3. Is reception of the Holy Spirit necessary to identification with the body of Christ?

Acts 1:5	*Acts 10:43-48*	*Eph. 2:18-22*
Acts 2:1-4,38	*1 Cor. 12:13*	*Summarize.*
Acts 8:15-17	*Eph. 1:13-14*	

   B. In what ways may the word *church* be used?

1. Of believers meeting in a home?

Rom. 16:5   *Col. 4:15*

2. Of believers in a city?

Acts 8:1   *Acts 13:1*   *Col. 1:2*

3. Of believers in a larger area?

Acts 9:31 ("church" is singular)   *1 Cor. 16:19*

4. Of all believers on earth at a given time (Universal church)?

1 Cor. 1:2   *1 Cor. 7:17*   *1 Cor. 14:33,36*

1 Cor. 4:17   *1 Cor. 11:16*

5. Of all believers from all times (Invisible church)?

Eph. 3:10,21   *Heb. 12:23*

Eph. 4:4   *Summarize this section.*

C. Does the inner, spiritual church express itself in outward, organized institutions?

1. What offices were necessary to conduct the worship and work in local churches?

Acts 14:23   *1 Tim. 3:1-2*   *Tit. 1:5,7*

Acts 20:17,28   *1 Tim. 3:8*   *1 Pet. 5:1-2*

Phil. 1:1

2. What activities or responsibilities of local churches required some organization?

Acts 2:41-42   *1 Cor. 5:13*   *Acts 20:7*

Acts 13:1-3   *Rom. 16:17*   *2 Cor. 8:1-9*

Acts 14:27   *3 Jn. 10*   *2 Cor. 9:6-7*

Acts 18:24-28   *1 Cor. 14:34*   *1 Tim. 5:9*

2 Cor. 3:1   *1 Cor. 16:2*

3. Is there biblical support for organized activities of believers on levels beyond the local church such as state, national and international churches or councils of churches? Was this the role of bishops? Are there apostles today? How would the four different types of churches (I. A.) interpret Acts 15:1-31?

D. Write out and memorize Heb. 10:24-25.

IV. *Your Conclusion*

As a result of this study how would you define the church spiritually and institutionally?

V. *Significance*

A. Have Christians today a right to limit the church to certain racial, national, geographical, economic or cultural levels?

B. If individual Christians cannot attain perfection in this life, may we expect to find perfect institutional churches?

C. Does the unity for which Christ prayed (Jn. 17) require institutional expression? If so, does it require or exclude unity with organizations which do not require biblical response to the Father's call, the Son's atonement or the Spirit's power?

D. Can a person fulfill his responsibilities to God, others and himself without participating in a local church?

Notes

[1] Andre de Bovis, "What Is the Church?" *Twentieth Century Encyclopedia of Catholocism,* XLVIII (New York: Hawthorn Books, 1961), pp. 96-126.

[2] J. W. C. Wand, *Anglicanism in History and Today* (London: Weidenfeld and Nicholson, 1961), pp. 1-45.

[3] Hans M. Mueller, "Church Polity," *The Encyclopedia of the Lutheran Church,* ed. by Julius Bodensieck, I (Minneapolis: Augsburg, 1965), pp. 519-526; Park Hays Miller, *Why I Am a Presbyterian* (New York: Thomas Nelson & Sons, 1956), pp. 72-89 and 98-106.

[4] Norman H. Maring and Winthrop S. Hudson, *A Baptist Manual of Polity and Practice* (Valley Forge: The Judson Press, 1953).

[5] Emil Brunner, *The Misunderstanding of the Church* (Philadelphia: The Westminster Press, 1953).

[6] Albert C. Outler, *The Christian Tradition and the Unity We Seek* (New York: Oxford University Press, 1957).

[7] Lewis Sperry Chafer, *Systematic Theology* (Dallas: Dallas Seminary Press, 1948), IV, pp. 36-143; VII, pp. 127-130.

[8] Walter Marshall Horton, *Christian Theology: An Ecumenical Approach* (New York: Harper & Brothers, 1955), pp. 204-243; Bruce Shelley, *Conservative Baptists* (Denver: Conservative Baptist Theological Seminary, 1960); J. Marcellus Kik: *Ecumenism and the Evangelical* (Philadelphia: The Presbyterian and Reformed Pub. Co., 1958).

20

Why does the church exist in the world?

I. *Background*

The world stands on the brink of disaster. Its need for the church is more evident than in more optimistic times. Christians know the Lord has called them out from the world to send them on an urgent mission. But many are confused as to the precise nature of their task. Is it social work or evangelism, or both? If both, what is their relationship?

A. Exactly what is the mission of the church to the world?

1. Some say that the church is sent into the world to transform the institutions and structures of society. The church cannot be satisfied with an otherworldly individualism or an acceptance of the status quo as providentially ordained. In different ways in different situations the church

must support whatever political system best achieves certain humane objectives. No distinction is made between those inside and outside the circle of salvation. (Liberals)[1]

2. Others seek to bring outsiders into the circle of salvation by participation in society. Evangelism is "Anything the Church may do which has as its ultimate end the winning of men and women to Christ and the winning of Christians to deepened commitment" (Charles Templeton). All Christians must actively participate in the affairs of the world like missionaries in foreign cultures. Believers should "go native" in everything except faith and morals. The Christian's witness need not be verbalized as the gospel makes its total impact upon the "worlds" of labor, leisure, education, government, and even ecclesiastical institutions. (Neo-evangelicals?)[2]

3. In direct contrast others insist, "Evangelism is not everything we do. One might conceivably spend all his time doing good and never evangelize. Moral righteousness is not evangelism. One never evangelizes until he stands directly before the heart's door of a sinner and clearly confronts him with the Gospel of Christ." (Fundamentalists)[3]

4. Another position suggests that everything Christians do is not evangelism, but works of loving service indirectly produce a climate conducive to evangelism. Evangelization as such is always a declaration of the gospel. However, that declaration may fall on deaf ears if the Christian church exists to be served rather than to lay down its life in service to a needy world. (Evangelicals)[4]

B. Who is responsible for evangelization of the lost?

1. Not the organized church, but individual Christians must win the lost. The world, not the church, is the sphere in which evangelism takes place. The world is not coming to the church. Therefore, individual Christians must take the good news to the world.[5]

2. Others say the true agent of evangelism is the church. Every member has a part to play, and the church may use professional evangelists and missionaries. But the policy, activity and worship of the local church must be evangelistic.[6]

3. A third view suggests that personal evangelism is the responsibility of every follower of Christ, whereas mass evangelism is the primary responsibility of local churches and gifted evangelists. Both individuals and churches in all that they do should endeavor to make such an impact upon the world that people will listen to the gospel when it is proclaimed.[7]

II. *Problem*

Which of the views concerning the Christian mission to the world is most faithful to Scripture? (To be answered in IV only after examining the evidence in III)

III. *Procedure*

Answer questions raised by the alternatives from your study of the Bible.

A. What is the believer's relation to people of the non-Christian world?

1. Is the believer to be distinct from the world morally and spiritually?

1 Jn. 2:15-16	*Jas. 4:4*
Jas. 1:27	*1 Jn. 5:4b*

2. Is the Christian nevertheless sent into the world wisely to participate in its affairs? In what ways?

Jn. 17:18	*Mt. 10:42*	*1 Cor. 10:31-33*
Mt. 5:14-16	*Lk. 10:27-37*	*Gal. 6:10*
Mt. 9:10-13	*1 Jn. 3:17-18*	*Tit. 2:7-8*
Lk. 7:34-35	*Rom. 13:8-14*	*Tit. 3:8*

3. In relation to the governments of the world, what are the Christian's responsibilities and rights?

Mk. 12:13-17	*Acts 22:22-29*	*1 Pet. 2:13-17*
Acts 16:35-40	*Rom. 13:1-7*	*Rev. 13:1-18*

B. Does New Testament evangelism require verbal presentations of the gospel to the world? (The Greek noun from which the English "evangel" comes, *euaggelion*, in all its 76 occurrences in the New Testament is translated gospel (KJ). The verb, *euaggelizō* is rendered: declare to, preach unto, bring glad tidings, bring good tidings, declare glad tidings unto, preach, preach the gospel, or have the gospel preached. Similarly *kataggellō* means tell thoroughly, *laleō* speak and *kērussō* proclaim, herald, cry.)

1. What message was declared, what gospel believed?

1 Cor. 15:1-4	Acts 10:36-43	1 Cor. 1:23
Acts 17:3	Jn. 1:12 with 1:1,14	1 Cor. 10:9,10
Acts 2:36	1 Jn. 4:1-3	Acts 17:18
Acts 5:42	Rom. 3:25	Gal. 1:8-9

2. What does the gospel imply concerning God?

Heb. 11:6	Rom. 1:17
Jn. 3:16	Rom. 3:21-26

3. What does the gospel imply concerning man?

Rom. 3:10-20,23	Eph. 2:1-4,12-13	Summarize this section.

4. What types of verbal presentations may be utilized?

Acts 9:29	Acts 17:18-34	2 Cor. 5:19-20
Acts 14:14	Rom. 15:18-19	Col. 1:28
Acts 17:2 (cf. 17:17;	1 Cor. 9:19-23	Jas. 5:19
18:4,11; 19:8-9; 24:25)		Summarize.

5. What attitudes accompany evangelistic discourse?

Rom. 1:14-16	1 Cor. 13	Col. 4:5-6
1 Cor. 9:16,19,23-27	2 Cor. 5:11-12,14,20	Summarize.

6. Who is to be evangelized?

Acts 4:8,10	Acts 10:45	Eph. 3:8-9
Acts 5:14; 8:12	Acts 26:22	Summarize.
Acts 6:7	Rom. 1:14,16	

7. Where is the good news to be heard?

Mt. 28:19	Acts 8:4,40	Rom. 15:20
Lk. 24:47	Acts 17:17,22	Summarize.
Acts 1:8		

C. Who is responsible for speaking evangelistically? Apostles only? Pastors in services only? Individual believers and not ministers? All believers and officers in the churches?

Mt. 28:19	*Acts 13:1-3*	*2 Tim. 4:5*
Acts 1:2,8,22	*Acts 14:27*	*1 Pet. 3:1*
Acts 8:1,4	*Acts 15:35*	*1 Pet. 3:15*
Acts 8:25	*2 Tim. 2:2*	*Summarize.*
Acts 11:20		

D. Write out and memorize Gal. 6:10 and 1 Cor. 9:22.

IV. *Your Conclusion*
Sum up in your words the mission of the church to the world and indicate who is responsible for fulfilling it.

V. *Significance*
A. In what ways can you help create a climate conducive to the evangelization of such people as the policemen or other officials of your city, state and nation?

B. Should you use the same approach in speaking to each person you seek to win to Christ?

C. Should the responsibility of world evangelization be left to professional missionaries and mission societies?

Notes

[1]John C. Bennett, ed., *Christian Social Ethics in a Changing World* (New York: Association Press, 1966), pp. 181-285.

[2]Sherwood Wirt, "The Young Turks of Evangelism," *Christianity Today*, IV (May 23, 1960), 691-694.

[3]C. E. Autry, *Basic Evangelism* (Grand Rapids: Zondervan, 1959), p. 27.

[4]J. Oliver Buswell, Jr., *A Systematic Theology of the Christian Religion*, I (Grand Rapids: Zondervan, 1962), pp. 344-429; David O. Moberg, *Inasmuch: Christian Social Responsibility in the Twentieth Century* (Grand Rapids: Wm. B. Eerdmans, 1965).

[5]C. Stacey Woods, "Is the Church the Center of Evangelism?" *Eternity*, IX (September 1958), 11-13.

[6]A. Skevington Wood, "The Church and Evangelism," *Christianity Today*, I (February 4, 1957), 15-17.

[7]Carl F. H. Henry and W. Stanley Mooneyham, eds., *One Race, One Gospel, One Task: World Congress on Evangelism, Berlin 1966*, II (Minneapolis: World Wide Publications, 1967), pp. 341-509.

21

Do Christians need the church?

I. *Background*

Many discerning people have become disenchanted with the institutional church. Is it imperative for healthy Christian living? Can we not be as good Christians without the endless meetings involved in planting and promoting churches? Answers to such questions are diverse and strong.

A. Some would destroy the institutional church. Ecclesiastical ritual has become a drag. Ecclesiastical language belonged to another century. There seems to be no appreciable difference between the views of church members and society as a whole. A church of value only for winning hockey games and gaining advantages in business does not deserve support. Dismiss the clergy, throw out the Bible, and tear down the edifices. Let Christians abandon a fixed set of rigid principles

and give themselves in love to real people. (Anti-institu-
tionalists)[1]

B. Others would endeavor to retain the church for insufficient and even unworthy reasons. It is an impressive place to
be married and buried. It is a harmless place for the children
when you want to get them out of the house on Sunday
morning. It may serve as a social club or an entertainment
center for civilians. In the church people can ease their con-
sciences by paying others to do their religious duties. (Some
suburbanites)[2]

C. Christians need the church, others suggest, as a vital
agency through which to express their love for God and each
other and to fulfill sharable objectives. (1) The church publicly baptizes the believer portraying his decisive revolt
against the tyranny of sin and commitment to the Lordship
of Christ. (2) The church provides for the believer's lifelong
learning of apostolic doctrine. (3) The church stimulates loving fellowship with others on the basis of common faith in
Jesus Christ, not educational, racial or social status. (4) The
church supplies a responsible observance of the Lord's
Supper signifying the believer's continued identification with
the crucified and risen Lord. (5) The church encourages the
believer's participation in united prayer. (6) The church
trains each member in the use of his spiritual gifts for the
benefit of all members. (7) Finally, the church helps each
believer fulfill the privileges and responsibilities of his priest-
hood. (Advocates of church renewal)[3]

II. *Problem*
How should a Christian view his church? Which view best
expresses the biblical reasons why a Christian needs the
church? (To be answered in IV)

III. *Procedure*
Answer from the written Word questions suggested by the

various partial and distorted perspectives of the church.

A. Is the believer, baptized into the body of Christ by the Holy Spirit, also to be publicly baptized into the fellowship of the church?

Mt. 28:19	*Acts 9:18*	*Rom. 6:3*
Acts 2:41	*Acts 10:47-48*	*Gal. 3:27-28*
Acts 8:12	*Acts 16:15,33*	*Summarize.*
Acts 8:36	*Acts 18:8*	

B. Is every Christian to enjoy lifelong learning in the church?

Mt. 28:19-20	*Col. 3:16*	*Eph. 4:11-16*
Acts 2:42	*1 Cor. 14:31*	*Summarize.*

C. Is every believer to share in the fellowship of the church? What may that include?

Acts 2:42	*Phil. 1:5*	*1 Jn. 1:6-7*
2 Cor. 8:4	*Phil. 2:1-3*	*Summarize.*
Gal. 2:9	*1 Jn. 1:3*	

D. Is the believer's continual union with Christ (and others who are his) to be represented in orderly participation in the Lord's table?

Mt. 26:26-27	*1 Cor. 10:14-17*	*1 Cor. 11:17-33*
Lk. 22:14-20	*1 Cor. 10:21*	*Summarize.*
Acts 2:42		

E. Is every believer to participate in the prayer meetings of the church?

Acts 2:42	*Acts 12:12*	*Acts 14:23*
Acts 4:24-31	*Acts 13:1-3*	*Summarize.*
Acts 6:6		

F. Are only a few church members gifted to minister to others or is every member gifted to serve the whole church?

Rom. 12:3-8	*1 Cor. 12:14-18*	*1 Pet. 4:10*
1 Cor. 12:7	*1 Cor. 12:25-26*	*Summarize.*

G. Are just a few Christians priests, or are all believers priests who through Christ's once-for-all sacrifice may intercede for others before God's throne, offer praise for God's mercy, and live a holy life? What, in fact, are the believers' privileges and responsibilities as priests?

1 Tim. 2:5   *Heb. 10:18-22*   *Rev. 1:5-6*

Heb. 4:15-16   *Heb. 13:15*   *Rev. 5:10; 20:6*

Heb. 10:10-12   *1 Pet. 2:5,9*   *Summarize.*

H. Write out and memorize Acts 2:41-42.

IV. *Your Conclusion*

Sum up in your own words the most important reasons why the believer needs the church and the church needs the believer.

V. *Significance*

A. Is the church a voluntary society in the sense that a believer may choose not to join it if he does not care to?

B. Does the phrase "full time Christian service" imply that those not so called are exempt from carrying out the mission of the church to itself and to the world?

C. How can we avoid a split-level fellowship between clergy and laity? What is the distinctive role of ordained pastors? In what respects are they no different from the rest of the people of God?

Notes

[1] Pierre Berton, *The Comfortable Pew* (Philadelphia: J. B. Lippincott Co., 1965); James Kavanaugh, *A Modern Priest Looks at His Outdated Church* (New York: Trident Press, 1967).

[2] Popular uses of the church by people for their own ends.

[3] William Kilbourn, ed., *The Restless Church: A Response to the Comfortable Pew* (Philadelphia: J. B. Lippincott Co., 1965), esp. pp. 75-79; D. Elton Trueblood, *The Incendiary Fellowship* (New York: Harper and Row, 1967); D. Elton Trueblood, *The Company of the Committed* (New York: Harper and Row, 1961); Robert A. Raines, *New Life in the Church* (New York: Harper and Row, 1961).

PART VIII

the hope of the church

22

Will Christ return to reign on this earth?

I. *Background*

Through the centuries great men have worked, bled and died to establish peace with justice. They fought the first World War to end all wars. Soon, however, a far worse debacle enveloped the nations. And still there is no peace. The cold war persists and limited hot wars ignite.

Will the nations ever secure a righteous and permanent peace? Christians pray for the rulers and support every valid program for peace. But Christians know that lasting peace is precluded by the deceitfulness of sinful hearts. The age-long quest of the nations can only be fulfilled by the help of Christ. Christians differ, however, on the way the Lord brings peace.

A. According to some Christ will never return to reign

over the earth. Christ's peace-bringing rule (kingdom) is only inward and spiritual. All biblical teaching about Christ's second coming and millennial kingdom is understood, not literally of the future, but existentially of present experience. Reinterpreted (remythologized), the doctrine of last things is realized here and now in Christians' hearts. Objective peace on earth will never be attained, but in the midst of turmoil and tragedy individuals may experience peace. (Many contemporary theologians)[1]

B. Others, agreeing that Christ's kingdom is primarily spiritual here and now, nevertheless believe in a literal return of Christ. But there will be *no* literal millennium. Millennial passages apply to the present reign of the Lord over his own, or to the eternal state in the new heavens and earth. The conclusion of this present evil age will feature Christ's return, the resurrection of all men and one final judgment. (Amillennialists)[2]

C. Christ literally returns to earth *after* a long period of peace brought to pass by the success of missionary efforts. As Christians continue to preach the gospel in the power of the Holy Spirit, the great majority of people in the world will be Christianized. Peace naturally follows this universal acknowledgement of Christ's lordship. Following the millennium will be Christ's return, the resurrection of all men and the final judgment. (Postmillennialists)[3]

D. Some anticipate Christ's literal return *before* his literal rule over all the earth. Only the Jewish aspects of the millennium are figurative, for at his first coming Christ forever abolished the distinction between Jew and Gentile. Israel may be converted, but is not prominent. Christ's present headship of the church and his coming rule of the nations are very similar. At his return the just are raised and judged. Only after the millennium will the wicked be raised and judged. (Historic premillennialists)[4]

E. Others take literally, not only Christ's return and subsequent reign, but also the prominence of Jewish aspects in his kingdom. These expect a restored Jewish nation with its twelve tribes, Christ ruling on the throne of David at Jerusalem, the fulfillment of blessings promised to Israel in the Old Testament and the reinstatement of worship by sacrifices. Christ's present headship of the church and his coming rule of the nations are very different. As in historic premillennialism there is not one general resurrection and judgment, but two separated by the 1000 year reign of Christ. (Dispensational premillennialists)[5]

F. A third type of premillennialism combines elements of the other two. Christ now reigns in the lives of those who recognize him as Lord and he will literally return to earth prior to the millennium. In agreement with historical premillennialists, Christ's 1000 year reign will continue the spiritual oneness of Jew and Gentile in Christ. Spiritually, Christ's present and future Lordship are similar. But in agreement with dispensational premillennialists, Christ's 1000 year reign is administered outwardly, not like a church with pastors and deacons, but like the Jewish nation with its king. Christ's present and future rules are quite different institutionally. The prominence of Israel is merely functional. (Some recent premillennialists)[6]

II. *Problem*
Which view of Christ's kingdom expresses the teaching of the greatest amount of Scripture with the fewest difficulties? (To be answered in IV only after examining the evidence in III)

III. *Procedure*
Subject these issues to the scriptural norm.
    A. Is there any sense in which Christ's redemptive kingdom is already realized in the hearts and lives of believers?

Jn. 3:3-7	*Acts 28:23,31*	*Col. 1:13*
Acts 19:8	*Rom. 14:17*	*Summarize.*

B. Is there also a future sense of Christ's kingdom which is not yet realized throughout the earth?

Isa. 11:9   *Ps. 22:27*   *Rev. 20:4*

Jer. 31:34   *Mal. 1:11*   *Summarize.*

C. Is the future rule of Christ identical with the eternal state after the creation of the new heavens and earth? Or is the millennial reign (Rev. 20:1-4) on this present earth and prior to the new heavens and earth (Rev. 21:1)? Are Revelation 20 and 21 in chronological order?

Ps. 22:27   *Zech. 14:9*

Isa. 11:9   *Summarize.*

D. Will Christ come after the church has Christianized the majority of people in the world? Or when Christ returns will unbelief and rebellion be prominent?

Mt. 24:3-31   *2 Tim. 3:1-5*   *Rev. 19:11-16*

Mt. 24:37-39   *2 Tim. 4:3-4*   *Summarize.*

Lk. 18:8   *2 Pet. 3:3-4*

E. If the millennium is not begun by the Christianization of the world, is it initiated by Christ's prior personal return? Does the return of Christ (Rev. 19:11-21) precede the millennial reign (Rev. 20:1-6)?

Zech. 14:1-11   *Acts 3:19-21*   *Rev. 19:11–20:7*

Jer. 23:5-6   *Rom. 11:25-26*   *Summarize.*

F. Do others reign with Christ?

Lk. 22:28-30   *2 Tim. 2:11-12*   *Summarize.*

1 Cor. 6:2-3   *Rev. 5:10*

G. Are two distinct resurrections separated by the 1000 year reign?

Rev. 20:4-5   *Acts 4:2**   *Summarize.*

Lk. 14:14   *Phil. 3:11**

Lk. 20:35-36*   **("of" = "out from among")*

H. Are Jew and Gentile one in Christ so that no spiritual distinction could be maintained between them during the millennium?

Rom. 10:12   *Col. 3:11*   *Gal. 3:28*

I. Are animal sacrifices forever done away by the one sacrifice of Christ?
Heb. 9:28–10:14

J. Is Israel as a literal nation, however, to enjoy a restoration as an instrument of God to bring even greater blessing to the world? (Does the spiritual unity of male and female, Gal. 3:28, exclude the husband's distinctive role as head of the wife, Eph. 5:23?)

Rom. 11:11-12,15	*Zech. 14:2,4,11*	*Acts 1:6*
Rom. 11:25-26	*Lk. 1:32-33*	*Summarize.*
Mic. 3:8–4:4	*Lk. 22:29-30*	

K. Write out and memorize Rev. 20:4-5.

IV. *Your Conclusion*
Explain your view of scriptural teaching on Christ's return to rule the world in peace.

V. *Significance*
A. If Christians cannot really hope to convert the whole world, have they any less responsibility to preach the gospel to every creature?

B. Although universal peace may not be permanent until Jesus returns, should Christians fail to pray and work for it?

C. Would a millennium of peace with justice on this earth be a fitting climax to God's purposes in the world and an appropriate transition (gateway) to the eternal state?

Notes

[1] Emil Brunner, *Eternal Hope* (Philadelphia: The Westminster Press, 1954); Rudolph Bultmann, *Theology of the New Testament* (New York: Charles Scribner's Sons, 1951, 1955), I, pp. 329-330; II, pp. 75-92.

[2] Floyd E. Hamilton, *The Basis of Millennial Faith* (Grand Rapids: Wm. B. Eerdmans, 1952), pp. 35-162.

[3] Loraine Boettner, *The Millennium* (Philadelphia: The Presbyterian and Reformed Pub. Co., 1958); A. H. Strong, *Systematic Theology* (Philadelphia: The Judson Press, 1907), pp. 1010-1015.

[4] J. J. Van Oosterzee, *Christian Dogmatics,* II (New York: Scribner, Armstrong & Co., 1874), pp. 798-801; D. H. Kromminga, *The Millennium* (Grand Rapids: Wm. B. Eerdmans, 1948).

[5] John F. Walvoord, *The Millennial Kingdom* (Findlay, Ohio: Dunham Pub. Co., 1959); J. Dwight Pentecost, *Things To Come* (Findlay, Ohio: Dunham Pub. Co., 1958), pp. 427-546.

[6] Robert D. Culver, *Daniel and the Latter Days* (Chicago: Moody Press, 1954), pp. 1-90 and 191-213; Gordon R. Lewis, "Dispensationalism, Covenant Theology and Pretribulationalism," *Biblical Studies* (Denver: Conservative Baptist Theological Seminary, 1966), Part I, mimeographed; published in *Bibliotheca Sacra,* CXXV (April-June 1968), 129-138; Rene Paché, *The Return of Jesus Christ* (Chicago: Moody Press, 1955), pp. 379-435.

23

When will believers meet Christ in the air?

I. *Background*

Among events clustered around Christ's return, none has aroused more curiosity than his "catching up" of believers to meet him in the air (1 Thess. 4:16-17). All who accept a literal second coming believe the "rapture" will happen. The question is when.

No one should set a date! But one cannot think about events such as Christ's earthly rule, a great tribulation (Mt. 24:21) and a rapture without placing them in some order.

The Bible, however, does not list these eschatological events chronologically. Any schedule is a matter of inference from scattered bits of evidence. Consequently, writers from every persuasion plead for freedom to differ on this issue. But it cannot be ignored. Should Christians prepare to face the world-wide devastation of the great tribulation? Or before it begins will they be caught up to be with Christ?

A. Some Christians place the rapture after the millennium which they think will be brought in by the church. Then Satan will be loosed for a little season, there will be great tribulation and the saints will be caught up to meet Christ. Christians now anticipate neither the tribulation nor the rapture, but peace for a thousand years. (Postmillennialists)[1]

B. Believers will meet Christ in the air only after terrible persecution from the antichrist who will rise to great power at the end of our age. As Christ returns to the battle of Armageddon Christians are caught up to meet him. Only then is his wrath poured out on the ungodly. These events could develop in the believer's lifetime. (Amillennialists)[2]

C. Among premillennialists four views prevail:

1. Christians may expect to meet Christ at the end of the great seven year period of tribulation. They should prepare for much suffering at the hands of the antichrist, but they will be preserved from God's wrath. Then, having met their returning king in the air, they shall immediately come back with him to reign in righteousness. At any time this complex of events could begin so that Christians might meet Christ in seven years. (Recent post-tribulationists)[3]

2. Believers will meet Christ in the middle of the tribulation. Having suffered at the hands of the ungodly for three and a half years, they will be with Christ during the last three and one-half years—the great tribulation. Then they will return with Christ to reign. Christians should prepare for unparalleled suffering, but may expect to meet their Lord in three and one-half years. (Mid-tribulationists)[4]

3. Although the tribulation takes place first, the rapture may occur at any moment. Man cannot identify the tribulation's beginning, middle or end. At any time its end may potentially be present, and believers be caught up to meet Christ. That same day Christ pours out his wrath on the

ungodly, and returns with believers to reign. Believers then, may meet Christ at any moment. (Historical post-tribulationists)[5]

4. The rapture occurs at any moment before the seven years of tribulation. The removal of the church marks the end of the times of the Gentiles and Israel's trust in Christ. Institutionally, the tribulation like the millennium, features no local churches, but a restored Israelite nation. The abomination of desolation takes place in the Jerusalem temple. The 144,000 servants of God sealed for protection are Jews. Believers now may expect to meet Christ before this identifiable period of time begins. (Pre-tribulationists)[6]

II. *Problem*

Which view accounts for most of the evidence with the fewest difficulties? (To be answered in IV only after examining the evidence in III)

III. *Procedure*

Answer crucial questions from examination of the scriptural data.

A. Will a great adversary of God arise, usurp Christ's place and persecute those who will not worship him?

2 Thess. 2:1-4	*Dan. 9:26-27*	*Rev. 13:11-18*
Mt. 24:15	*Rev. 13:1-10*	*Summarize.*
Dan. 7:24-25		

B. Will God pour out his wrath upon ungodly men "who dwell upon the earth"? Specify acts of God beyond all human control or instrumentality.

Rev. 6:16-17	*Rev. 16:1,19*	*Rev. 13:8,12,14*
Rev. 11:18-19	*Rev. 19:15*	*Rev. 14:6*
Rev. 14:19	*Rev. 3:10*	*Rev. 17:8*
Rev. 15:1,7	*Rev. 11:10*	*Summarize.*

C. Could we today be at the end of such a period of tribulation? Refer to verses in A. and B.

D. How long is the tribulation? Is it the seventieth unit of seven years each mentioned by Daniel?

Dan. 9:24-27 (Mt. 24:15)   *Rev. 12:13-14 (Dan. 7:25)*

Rev. 13:5   *Rev. 12:6*   *Summarize.*

E. Why do recent post-tribulationists think the church will go through the entire period of tribulation?

Mt. 24:29-31 ("elect" interpreted as the church)

2 Thess. 2:1-3

Rev. 20:4-6 (first resurrection)

Events predicted prior to Christ's return ruled out an any-moment expectancy for the apostles:

Jn. 21:18,19   *Acts 1:8*

Mt. 24:2   *Summarize.*

F. Why do mid-tribulationists think the church is raptured after the first half of the tribulation?

Rev. 10:7 ("mystery"   *Rev. 11:15-18*

interpreted as   *cf. 1 Cor. 15:52*

the church)   *cf. 1 Thess. 4:13-18*

G. Why do historical post-tribulationists and pre-tribulationists believe that Christians could be caught up to meet Christ at any moment?

Mt. 24:36—25:13   *1 Cor. 1:7*   *Jas. 5:7-8*

Mk. 13:32-36   *Phil. 4:5*   *Jude 21*

Lk. 12:36-40   *1 Thess. 1:9-10*   *Summarize.*

Rom. 8:19,23,25   *Tit. 2:12-13*

H. Are the saints and the elect on earth during the tribulation members of institutional churches or of the restored Israelite nation?

Mt. 24:15-31   *Rev. 7:3-8*   *Rev. 16:6*

See Isa. 45:4   *Rev. 13:7-10*   *Rev. 17:6*

See Isa. 65:22   *Rev. 14:12*   *Rev. 18:24*

See Rom. 11:5,28   *Rev. 14:1-5*   *Summarize.*

I. Does Rev. 3:10 refer to (1) the first century church at Philadelphia, Asia Minor only or to (2) the Philadelphian church and similar churches until the time of universal tribulation? On the last phrase of 3:10 ("those who dwell upon the earth") see Rev. 11:10; 13:8,12,14; 14:6; 17:8.

Does Rev. 3:10 teach that believers will be preserved through tribulation or kept from the period (hour) of tribulation?

J. Write out and memorize Rev. 3:10.

IV. *Your Conclusion*
When do you expect believers to meet Christ in the air? Why?

V. *Significance*
A. On any view of the rapture need a Christian fear the wrath of God?

B. Should a Christian's fear of persecution determine his doctrine of the rapture?

C. What practical implications for daily Christian living does your position on the rapture involve?

Notes

[1]Loraine Boettner, *The Millennium* (Philadelphia: The Presbyterian and Reformed Pub. Co., 1958), pp. 14-18.

[2]Floyd E. Hamilton, *The Basis of Millennial Faith* (Grand Rapids: Wm. B. Eerdmans, 1952), pp. 35-37.

[3]George Ladd, *The Blessed Hope* (Grand Rapids: Wm. B. Eerdmans, 1956).

[4]J. Oliver Buswell, Jr., *A Systematic Theology of the Christian Religion*, II (Grand Rapids: Zondervan, 1962), pp. 445-450 and 491-493; Rene Paché, *The Return of Jesus Christ* (Chicago: Moody Press, 1955), pp. 109-135.

[5]J. Barton Payne, *The Imminent Appearing of Christ* (Grand Rapids: Wm. B. Eerdmans, 1962).

[6]E. Schuyler English, *Re-Thinking the Rapture* (Travelers Rest, South Carolina: Southern Bible Book House, 1954); Gordon R. Lewis, "Dispensationalism, Covenant Theology and Pretribulationalism," *Biblical Studies* (Denver: Conservative Baptist Theological Seminary, 1966), Part II, pp. 7-15 mimeographed, part of which is in *Bibliotheca Sacra*, CXXV (July-September 1968), 216-226.

24

What happens after death?

I. *Background*

No escape avails. Sooner or later—unless Jesus Christ returns first—we shall die. In spite of our most elaborate attempts to avoid the subject, we inevitably think about our death and eternal destiny. From such considerations emerge most varied opinions. The views of man (Study Guide 10) are influential here.

A. Believing only what they see, some think death ends all. Beyond the grave we have nothing to fear and nothing to enjoy. No soul survives. The deceased are totally annihilated. (Naturalists, materialists)[1]

B. Others, even on the ground of scientific observation, say death does not end all. "Science has found that nothing can disappear without a trace. Nature does not know extinc-

tion. All it knows is transformation." If true of more insignif-
icant parts of the universe, how much more true of man?
(Wernher Von Braun)[2]

C. Some, on philosophical ground, hold an impersonal immortality. The dew drop slips into the shining sea; while
losing its identity it remains. At death we lose our individ-
uality as we are absorbed into the infinite Whole (God, The
Absolute). (Spinoza, Hegel, pantheists)[3]

D. After death, some religions assert, the eternal soul
occupies another body. Hundreds of thousands of such trans-
migrations are necessary before release from the realm of
birth and death. Whether the succeeding incarnations are of
higher or lower forms of animal or human life depends on the
good and evil in this life. The inexorable moral law of *karma*
provides no forgiveness. (Hindus and Buddhists)[4]

E. We continue gradual moral development in the vicinity
of our physical life and death. No distant heaven or hell
separates the dead from the living. The dead are invisible to
the physical senses, but not to minds attuned to psychic
force. Evidence for this view is alleged from communications
with the dead and extra-sensory perception. (Spiritualists)[5]

F. Many who accept personal immortality deny eternal
punishment. Eventually all men will be saved. (Universalists)
If some remain incorrigible after a second chance or a purga-
tory, they will be annihilated. (Conditional immortality)[6]

G. Others deny an immortality of the soul, but believe in
a resurrection. Alleging that conscious existence of the soul
without the body is an ancient Greek idea, not a biblical one,
they teach that the soul sleeps between death and the resurrection. The whole man—body and soul—dies; the whole man
is raised from the dead. (Jehovah's Witnesses, Latter-day
Saints, Seventh-day Adventists, some contemporary theologians)[7]

H. During his irrepeatable life on earth each person determines his eternal destiny. At death the soul consciously exists

in the presence of God or in torment until the body is raised. Then the whole man, on the authority of Scripture, exists eternally in a condition determined by God's just judgment. Those who suffer are punished only to the degree of divine truth they refused. Those who are glorified with Christ receive his inheritance by faith as a gift. God also recognizes their stewardship of his grace. They dwell in the newly created heavens and earth, not a merely spiritual "heaven." (Orthodox Christians)[8]

II. *Problem*
Which doctrine of the after life most faithfully states the biblical teaching? (To be answered in IV only after examining the evidence in III)

III. *Procedure*
From your study of relevant Scripture answer questions raised by the various views.

A. Does death end all, or is there life beyond the grave?

Ps. 23:4,6	*Rom. 8:38-39*	*Summarize.*
Eccl. 12:7	*(The other passages in*	
Lk. 23:43	*this study also apply here.)*	

B. After death are individuals absorbed into an impersonal Being, or do they retain their personal identities?

Mt. 17:1-4	*Rom. 2:3*	*(Passages in D.*
Lk. 9:30-33	*Heb. 12:23*	*also apply here.)*
Mt. 22:23-32		*Summarize.*

C. Does each soul go through a series of incarnations and deaths or just one life and death on this earth?
Heb. 9:26-27

D. Is a person's eternal destiny settled in a kind of purgatorial second chance after death or before his death?

Jer. 17:9-10	*Lk. 16:19-31*	*2 Cor. 5:10*
Mt. 13:36-45	*Jn. 12:48*	*Summarize.*
Lk. 9:23-26		

E. Between death and the resurrection of the body do both soul and body sleep, or does only the body sleep and the disembodied soul consciously experience either torment or Christ's presence?

| Lk. 16:22-31 | 2 Cor. 5:1-8 | 1 Thess. 4:14 |
| Lk. 23:43 | Phil. 1:23 | Summarize. |

F. Can bodies of those long dead be raised?

| Acts 26:8 | Jn. 11:39-44 | 2 Cor. 4:14 |
| Jn. 5:25-29 | 1 Cor. 15:12,20-23 | Summarize. |

G. What will resurrection bodies be like? List similarities to our present bodies and differences from our present bodies.

| Mt. 22:30 | Lk. 24:36-42 | 1 Cor. 15:35-58 |
| Mt. 28:9 | Jn. 20:24-28 | |

Does "flesh and blood" in 1 Cor. 15:50 forbid a bodily resurrection, or is "flesh and blood" an idiom for the natural realm as in Mt. 16:15-17?

Summarize.

H. What will be the eternal state of people who, persisting in their own righteousness, reject God's holy love? Are there degrees of punishment?

Mt. 11:21-24	Mt. 25:41,46	Rev. 20:14
Lk. 12:47-48	2 Thess. 1:8-9	Rev. 21:8
Mt. 10:28	Jude 1:7	Summarize.
Lk. 12:5	Rev. 14:10	

I. What conditions will be excluded from the eternal state of believers?

| Rev. 21:1,4,22 | Rev. 22:3,5 | Rev. 22:15 |
| Rev. 21:23,25 | Rev. 21:8,27 | Summarize. |

J. What conditions will be included in the eternal state of the redeemed?

Rev. 21:1 (See	Rev. 21:6,22; 22:1	Rev. 22:2,14
2 Pet. 3:7-13;	Rev. 21:11; 22:5	Rev. 22:3-4
Rom. 8:18-23)	Rev. 21:11-21	Rev. 22:5
Rev. 21:2,10	Rev. 21:27	Summarize.

K. Write out and memorize Rom. 8:18.

IV. *Your Conclusion*
Sum up in your own words major aspects of your conclusion concerning what follows death.

V. *Significance*
A. With what attitudes should a Christian face death?

B. What effects should your conclusion have upon your stewardship of life here and now?

C. Does happiness, in this life or the one to come, consist primarily in the abundance of things possessed, or in communion with God, service of others and renewal of ourselves?

Notes

[1] Corliss Lamont, *The Illusion of Immortality* (New York: G. P. Putnam's Sons, 1935).

[2] Wernher Von Braun, "Immortality," *This Week Magazine* (January 24, 1960), p. 2.

[3] Robert M. Hutchins, ed., *Great Books of the Western World* (Chicago: Encyclopedia Britannica, 1952), II, pp. 792-794; Spinoza, *Ethics*, Part V, Prop. 21-42, XXXI, pp. 458-463; Hegel, *Philosophy of Right*, Part III, par. 173 and 348, XLVI, pp. 61 and 111; *Philosophy of History*, XLVI, pp. 189, 212, 246-7, 254-5, 262-3, 274-5, 278-9 and 281-2.

[4] G. T. Manley and A. S. Neech, "Hinduism," *The World's Religions*, ed. by J. N. D. Anderson (London: Inter-Varsity Fellowship, 1950), pp. 107-110; David Bentley-Taylor, "Buddhism," *Ibid.*, pp. 123-126; J. Stafford Wright, *Man In the Process of Time* (Grand Rapids: Wm. B. Eerdmans, 1956), pp. 138-149.

[5] Joseph P. Whitwell, "After Death—What?" *What Is Spiritualism?* ed. by Emil C. Reichel (Milwaukee: National Spiritualist Association, n. d.), pp. 18-21; Ruth Montgomery, *A Search for the Truth* (New York: William Morrow Co., Bantam, 1968), pp. 219-235.

[6] *Seventh-Day Adventists Answer Questions on Doctrine* (Washington, D. C.: Review and Herald, 1957), pp. 509-609; Stewart D. F. Salmond, *The Christian Doctrine of Immortality* (Edinburgh: T. & T. Clark, 1913), pp. 473-524.

[7] *Let God Be True* (New York: Watchtower Bible and Tract Society, 1952), pp. 66-75; Oscar Cullmann, "Immortality or Resurrection?" *Christianity Today*, II (July 21, 1958), 3-6 and (August 18, 1958), 13-17.

[8] Harry Buis, *The Doctrine of Eternal Punishment* (Grand Rapids: Baker Book House, 1957); Wilbur M. Smith, *The Biblical Doctrine of Heaven* (Chicago: Moody Press, 1968).